PLUNDER LAND

Mark Newham

Published by MoriartiMedia.com

About the Author

During a thirty-year career as a print and broadcast journalist **Mark Newham**'s coverage of international affairs has appeared in almost every quality British newspaper, in international news magazines and on the BBC.

With foreign postings including Africa and China, Newham has combined journalism with media consultancy work for the United Nations, the World Bank and the European Union.

Plunderland is the third in a three-part series charting China's growing influence on the world. The first – *Limp Pigs* – was published in 2011 and ranked Number One in Amazon's censorship category for several weeks.
The BBC called it 'Unique... Inspiring...'

This was followed in 2014 by *Cometh the Yuan*, described by the Guardian newspaper as 'Beautifully rendered...
a cut above the rest.'

Mark Newham can (sometimes) be contacted through
mail@moriartimedia.com

To Nina

chapter one

Near-death experiences weren't supposed to be like this. Cerebral lockdown. Off-planet excursion. Sudden uncontrollable incontinence. That's how it should play out.

Not like this.

Not a train crash of thoughts so divorced from reality it left your man wondering if, like his faithful steed of twenty-something years, he'd finally gone over the edge.

Kearney knew he'd been close for some time. That's what this damned continent did to you. Every day it presented something new, something to test your mental metal. And every day for the best part of three decades Kearney had woken up wondering if this was it. If this was the tipping point day Africa had in mind for him.

Anyone flying overhead looking down on the lone Irishman squatting in the African wilderness dirt, eyes rolling in time to the gradually slowing rotation of his upturned vehicle's flailing wheels, his mind unable to focus on anything but the conundrum of why it was that you never saw Asians wearing sunglasses, would be hard pressed to say it wasn't.

So there it was. At least Kearney knew. Today was the day and that was that. There was no going back and now he had that settled Kearney thought he might as well make the most of it. It wasn't every day you were given total, unfettered freedom from rational thought. So…

'It's a true mystery,' he heard himself telling the wreckage. 'I mean, you'd never see a European without a decent pair of shades would you? They need them to protect against the glare of what Conrad laughably called the "dark" continent.

'And your average African? He'd kill for a pair to make him look cool or others feel uncomfortable.

'It's only the *Wahindis* who seem to have no interest in them. Why? Are they genetically immune to bright sunlight or something?'

Nah, he told the wreckage. That wasn't it. There had to be something more and Kearney thought he knew what. When everything every Asian he knew did was in some way connected to making a buck there had to be a commercial angle to it.

'They'd even sell their beloved cricket down the river if there was money in it,' he opined to his captive audience at the foot of the ravine.

But sunglasses? That was a weird one.

For a moment he paused, allowing the mental wheels to spin.

Then it came to him.

Of course. It was obvious when you thought about it. It was all about stopping the Chinese. Stopping them eating even further into traditional *Wahindi* interests in Africa. Non-Chinese Asian businesses were already being decimated by Chinese competition. Buying largely Chinese-made sunglasses would just be helping them take over completely.

* * *

Sunglasses? Asians? Fockin' China?

'Jayzuz fockin' Chroist!' yelled Kearney at the sky beating already bruised temples with bleeding fists. 'Get a fockin' grip will yer? If yer don't start focussing double fockin' quick yer double fockin' focked.'

Up to a point it worked. While the head banging hadn't

2

eradicated Kearney's bizarre train of thought entirely it had at least solved the issue of what had brought it on. The connection, he now saw, was his own pair of wrap-arounds. If he hadn't been wearing them as he'd careered over the ravine edge into the parched river bed below he'd more than likely have been blinded by the flying glass.

'Ah. Roight,' he mumbled to the lizard gawping at him from a nearby rock. 'Fock.'

Fock indeed, he thought, staring through the cloud of dust kicked up by his vehicle's plunge to watch Kilimanjaro's snow-capped summit gradually turning strawberry as the fireball sun banked to begin its regular evening bombing raid on Africa's highest peak.

It was a sight Kearney would have lapped up under normal circumstances, marvelling at one of nature's greatest sights.

But these weren't normal circumstances. Far from it. In his current predicament, the change in old Kili's colour and everything around it signalled the onset of something that brought dread to Kearney's heart.

Red dust, red sky, red earth, red devils on the wind and the wisps of scrubby vegetation stretching away towards Tsavo's shimmering horizon gradually turning crimson in the early evening light. Everything portended the rapid onset of night and the thought brought a shiver to a brow he now realised was dripping blood on to the scorched earth between his crooked knees.

Left unstaunched, Kearney knew it would soon be sending a message to every stalking beast within a five-mile radius that dinner was about to be served.

But on he sat, watching in fascination as the stain on the earth grew bigger and wondering how long it would take to gather a glass of his own claret so he could raise a toast to his new red world.

As long as it took for his own red mist to clear? It would eventually. He knew that. This wasn't the first time he'd travelled concussion road.

'Shame the same can't be said of red ink,' he grumbled to the lizard, unable to kick himself out of his low orbit around reality. 'If time alone could erase it from bank statements I'd still be on the road and within touching distance of a tall frosty one.'

But time, it seemed, didn't know what was being expected of it. The opposite in fact. The more of it there was, the more blood red the ink on his statements seemed to get and Kearney found himself thinking that this, at last, might be the final drop.

In view of his recently-executed excursion to the foot of the ravine, precipitous seemed an appropriate description of his financial position. Things had been bad before, but now... fock. How much it was going to cost to get the Millennium Falcon back on the road didn't bear thinking about.

It wasn't the labour cost that worried him. He and Ryan had the skills to piece her back together themselves. They'd done it how many times? But this time it was going to be genuine parts or nothing. No more cheap Chinese junk for him. He'd learned his lesson. It had, after all, been their use that'd not only landed him in his current predicament but were wholly to blame for the red ink tsunami now sweeping down on him from the direction of Barclays bank.

If only he'd listened to Ryan. If only he'd demanded money from the Chinese instead of stuff, he wouldn't be where he was now. But he hadn't. For once in his life he'd taken the long view and it was that decision that now looked destined to kill any hope the pair had of ever setting foot on Irish turf again.

'Fockin' Africa. Fockin' Chinese. Why did I ever have anything to do with either?'

Kearney knew why.

Africa was a bitch. A nark of a cow that made an addict out of all who crossed her path. Once you allowed her to wrap you in her octopus embrace you were done for. Struggling just made matters worse. You could never beat her, Kearney had long since realised, just hope you survived her.

Unless, Kearney's convulsing mind mused, you were Chinese. Somehow they'd found a way of staying aloof. Of simply treating Africa as a resource. How?

It was obvious when you thought about it. When the Chinese discovered Africa was an octopus their eyes lit up. Famed for eating anything with legs except the table, imagine their delight on encountering something with twice the usual number. Here was something that could feed the whole family. All one point four billion of the buggers.

It hadn't taken long for China to realise it and once they had the octopus's days were numbered. China's extended family descended on it to tear the animal apart.

And himself, Kearney mumbled ruefully. If only he'd taken the money. If only he'd done what Ryan said. If only he'd gone for genuine parts. If only…

'JAAAAY-ZUS!' Kearney yelled at the innocent lizard aping Kearney's third violent head shake in as many minutes. 'Get out! Get out! Get fockin' out! Got to fockin' focus! This is no time to be worrying about fockin' money!'

The lizard nodded sagely in agreement. In his considered opinion, with the smothering African night coming at him like a runaway train, the man squatting in the dirt yelling and beating his bleeding head with his fists should most definitely be focussing on an issue of rather greater urgency – which of the three was more likely to arrive first… the help, the brigands or the lions.

chapter two

Xi Ren felt a tear well in his eye as he looked at it. Right there, right in front of him, was a thing so bizarre it could only have been a roadkill victim on the path of evolutionary development. Xi knew the product of a natural order dead-end when he saw one. He had to deal with their modern day human equivalents every day of his life.

As anguished as he felt for the fossilised remains he'd just uncovered, the tear was more of remorse than sorrow. As irrational as he knew it to be, he always felt the need to apologise to anything he found entombed in the layers of rock he cracked open. He couldn't help the feeling of intrusion into the privacy of something that had lain undisturbed and unmolested for millions of years. Whenever it happened, the words 'grave' and 'robber' came readily to mind, refusing to be exorcised until he'd vocalised a sincere and heart-felt apology.

Xi knew the look his workmates exchanged on first hearing him muttering apologetically to just-discovered fossils would have consequences. The only surprise was that there was only one, and a not especially onerous one at that.

Although *mganga* hadn't been coined by them, Xi's fellow workers conferred the nickname on him with relish after looking up the translation of the Swahili word screeched by African kids on first encountering the crazy Chinese who talked to rocks.

'Witch doctor' fitted Xi perfectly. Here was a man who'd not only materialised out of nowhere, refusing point blank to disclose anything about himself, but had once regaled them with his theory about fossils not being as inanimate as they first appeared.

'Think about it,' he'd insisted as the group sat around the campfire one night. 'That little critter you're looking at could've been the last of its kind… ever. If, as our forebears believed, the spirits of the ancestors really do get passed on to those who come after them, then, if it is the last of its line, who's to say that that small creature isn't the ultimate receptacle of billions of accumulated ancestral spirits. Spirits which might just be prompted to take revenge on those who invaded their final resting place…'

Xi hadn't intended the theory to be taken seriously. It was just his way of testing the humour receptors of the other crew members, a robotic band of men he was pretty sure had been institutionalised into the brain dead state that anyone who'd had to undergo China's re-education and rehabilitation process inevitably ended up in.

His colleagues' collective response confirmed his darkest fears. As lifeless as the rocks they studied, their eyes told him that all he could expect for the duration of his time with them extended no further than the characterless interaction of those subjected to the systematic elimination of imagination, initiative and personality. Here, quite clearly, was a group of men crafted from the same institutional mould, mass produced to mechanically carry out the tasks demanded of them by the heartless system they served.

Xi surmised they hadn't started out that way. It was just the way those of lesser resistance to the Chinese state's persuasive charms ended up. Xi knew. He'd seen great men crushed. Humiliated into submission through being turned through three hundred and sixty degrees so often they eventually didn't know which way they were facing. It was the Party way and it worked. Even when such re-crafted former miscreants were released from their rehabilitation centres, their minds remained in incarceration. Even out here.

Most people, as Xi well knew, came to the great African beyond to escape, either permanently or for whatever time they were allowed away from their regular humdrum existences.

Not so for Xi and his fellow workers. For them there was no escape. When none of your team knew which was the one infiltrated into your ranks to keep an eye on the rest, you carried your own prison with you. When you didn't know who you were talking to you kept your nose clean and your thoughts to yourself… just as Xi had done for the past twenty-eight years after being convicted of the 'crime' of being in the wrong place at the wrong time.

Beijing's Tiananmen Square on the fourth of June 1989 to be precise. The day the tanks rolled in to crush the democracy movement taking root there.

* * *

The tear in Xi's eye wasn't just one of remorse. It was also one of recognition. Right there, right under his nose, was himself looking up at him.

'Take a good look, my friend,' said the unidentifiable entity in his hand. 'The only thing that separates you from me is breath. You are me plus pulse. That's what they've made sure you've become. A living fossil. You'll deny it, I know. But take a look around. Is that life you see before you?'

Xi raised his eyes to take in his surroundings. In one direction, an endless expanse of scrubby bush stretching away to the heat-shimmer distorted horizon. In the other, a distant grey-blue line of scorched earth hills breaching the surface like whales in formation, the whole panorama punctuated by nothing more than the occasional rotten tooth rocky outcrop or snake-infested termite mound. And in every direction not one lone thorn tree offering protection from the unforgiving sun.

A more inhospitable place Xi could hardly imagine and once he'd taken it all in he began to see what the fossil was getting at. Here was a place that all but the most hardy of Somali camel herders, fugitives from justice and the occasional gaggle of Chinese penance-servers would avoid. In other words, all except those who had no choice.

Although he had no evidence to prove it, Xi was pretty sure the penance-server description fitted every one of the men he'd been shipped off to work with, even the one infiltrated by the system into their ranks. Since no Chinese in his right mind would ever venture into such a place voluntarily he too must have earned the state's displeasure to warrant such an assignment – overseeing a group of miscreants dispatched to dig in the waterless north Kenya wastelands that served little purpose other than to provide a battleground for local tribal cattle rustling wars.

Who the system stoolie was though, Xi had no idea. Just that it wasn't him. He wouldn't be the one fingering one of his colleagues for letting word slip. It couldn't be. If word was to get out, Xi was determined it would be coming from him.

Payback. That's all he wanted. Payback for twenty-eight long years of being removed from the world for a crime he didn't commit. Payback which would come in the form of getting word to the outside world that China was homing-in on the geological holy grail.

With none outside his crew and the Chinese embassy in Nairobi knowing how close they were, Xi knew how the authorities who'd consigned him to this waterless grave would be reacting. They'd be rubbing their hands in anticipation of soon being in secret possession of something so rare it had achieved legendary status.

That, Xi had decided, was not going to happen. Well it would, but not in the way they wanted. They wouldn't be the only ones knowing it had happened. Very shortly, the *mganga* would be earning his nickname by magic-ing some highly unexpected news in the direction of a very surprised Irishman.

Very shortly, via his only contact with the outside world that world would be hearing of Beijing's latest acquisition – an almost mythical element which held the key to ensuring China's dream of achieving its ultimate ambition was delayed no longer... regaining its rightful place as undisputed master of the universe.

chapter three

His best yet. That's what it had to be. Pastor Gideon Kariuki felt good and he wanted everyone else to share it.

Well, nearly everyone. Not the godless or the infidel obviously. But almost everyone. Especially those who'd helped him arrive at the verge of securing all their futures and most definitely a place in paradise for himself.

So Kariuki was taking his time over this one. This, he'd decided, wouldn't be the usual florid outpouring of exhortations culled from past orations and padded out with well-worn passages from the scriptures. This time it had to have original content building to a glorious climactic finale in celebration of what it was he and his flock had achieved together.

Naturally he'd reserve a word or two for self-veneration. That was a given. But mostly it'd be about how selfless sacrifice to the cause could culminate in bringing riches to all true believers. Riches showered on them by the one true God. The one who, in His infinite wisdom, had created the world six thousand years earlier, had placed man irrevocably at the top of the food chain and had reserved a special place at His right hand for all who worshipped at the one true church. Kariuki's.

There was plenty of competition. Of that Kariuki was only too aware. But the church he'd founded had the edge. No question. The visitation that'd woken him not two hours after succumbing to his birthday indulgence left him in no doubt.

'Gideon,' boomed the unmistakeable voice of God in his head, 'if you want to save yourself, save others. Save them from themselves and be assured of everlasting piss.'

Head thumping and rigid with awe, Kariuki was suddenly wide awake. He'd heard of others receiving like visitations but had always put it down to simple-mindedness or the after-effects of psychological trauma.

Now he'd heard it himself he wasn't so sure. He was both well-educated and mentally well-balanced. Everyone said so. And anyway the word he'd received seemed so real. Well, all except the last. That must have been a mishearing.

* * *

For days after his enlightening, Kariuki wandered about in a dream. Distant and distracted and seeing new meaning in the flotilla of religious billboards making Nairobi's street signs unreadable, he was only shaken out of the reverie by his secretary.

Did he really intend that decimal point to go there? Was he really saying that the bank had gone from healthy profit to catastrophic loss overnight?

Once again Kariuki was wide awake. But for his secretary's diligence, the mistake could have cost him a lot more than his finance directorship. There was the value of his shares and his place on the board to think about. Deprived of these and he'd be deprived of the preferential loan treatment that gave him the means to live well beyond them.

At first, Kariuki chastised himself roundly for his stupidity. But then it came to him. Could the mistake have been divine intervention? Was it a wake-up call from the Almighty Himself? Had the Great Creator had a hand in manufacturing both the mistake and his secretary's noticing of it specifically to plant in Kariuki's mind the follow-up enlightenment he was now having?

God, reflected Kariuki, had told him to set up a church but not how to fund it. Was the decimal point error God's way of revealing how He wanted it done? Was He saying that the bank should put its profits to better use than simply making more money? If He was, how could the bank's depositors object? Their funds would be going towards doing the good works of the Lord God Himself.

And so it was that, thanks to Kariuki's second revelation and the generosity of those who'd placed their hard-earned cash at the disposal of one of Kenya's most trusted banks, Our Saviour's Church of Number One Good Samaritans had been born. A church, Kariuki reassured himself, whose 'investors' wouldn't regret their investment. God had given His word on that and Kariuki had no reason to doubt Him.

Or he hadn't until the day he'd awoken to the news that the world's banks had gone into meltdown and governments across the globe had had to step in to bail them out.

Erupting just days after 'arranging' the church's loan, the banking crash of 2008 saw Kariuki looking on in horror as bank after bank failed and the regulators began subjecting the world's financial sector to the sort of scrutiny normally reserved for Olympic drug cheats.

Would Kenya's banks emerge from it unscathed? More importantly, how long did he have before he was personally brought to book over the unconventional banking practice applied to the raising of funds for his church? Kariuki went almost white at the thought.

'Fear not,' came the voice of God in response to Kariuki's plea for guidance. 'They wouldn't dare.'

'Why not, Lord?'

'You're in Kenya, Gideon, a country so besotted with worship of Me that any questioning of church affairs is taken as a heinous blasphemy. So no, they won't be bothering you. They'd have the ultra-pious Kenyan people to answer to.'

In the years following the banking crisis God's confidence had looked well-founded. Not only had the regulators passed by on the other side but Kariuki's church had gone from strength to strength.

Then, almost a decade later, things changed. Under pressure from its aid donors, Kenya's government had no option but to accept independent financial scrutiny and Kariuki started sensing the vultures circling.

If God also sensed it, he wasn't saying and for the first time in his life Kariuki felt the cold knot of abandonment tighten round his neck. Had his God deserted him in his hour of greatest need? It was beginning to look that way.

As the dragnet closed in, Kariuki experienced two more firsts – resignation to the inevitable then abject genuflection to a higher power in appealing for mercy and forgiveness.

'O ye of little faith,' he chastised himself when the answer finally arrived. 'How could I ever have doubted You? How could I ever have thought You were too busy to help a poor wretch in his hour of need? Unforgiveable.'

* * *

How appropriate. The name of the man God had brought him to lead him out of the desert and into the promised land was Moses. Well, not lead exactly. More unwittingly provide him with the vehicle to make the trip. With what Moses had told him it was Kariuki who now saw himself as the real Moses. His parishioner's tip-off had provided Kariuki with the means of parting the financial equivalent of the Red Sea, guiding his loyal band of followers across the great monetary wasteland that lay beyond and delivering them safely to the land of milk, honey and *nyama choma*.

Well, to the outskirts at least. Just one more push and they were home free. The regulators would be off his back, the church and his flock would be saved and he'd have an escape route from the now wholly-discredited banking business. With what he now had in his possession, he'd not only be able to repay the loan, discreetly and in full, but distance himself from an institution on the brink of a very messy implosion.

As Kariuki mulled over how to impart the good news to his flock in his celebratory oratory he realised he had an important decision to make. Should he refer to specific individuals who'd made the celebration possible? Without people like Moses all their backs would be up against the wall. But then again, Moses wasn't really aware of how valuable the information had been. It'd taken the pastor himself to spot it.

So no, after much deliberation, Moses wouldn't be getting a special mention. If he did, Kariuki would be faced with having to go into detail and that would mean having to make reference to two other key players in the game whose influence on it Kariuki most certainly didn't want publicised.

Were it to become known that the final *coup de grâce* hinged on how things panned out between the Chinese and that scallywag Kearney, his flock might start shifting uneasily in their seats and that was the last thing Kariuki needed. Having the full confidence of what amounted to a private army was vital to the success of his mission to save their souls and, purely by coincidence of course, his.

chapter four

Contrary to the evidence staring him in the face, Kearney liked to consider himself a realist. A man with both feet planted firmly on the ground who took nothing for granted and had as much time for dreamers as the Chinese had for making durable car parts.

Those who knew him were minded to disagree. With a failure record to rival any of Africa's crash-prone banks, if ever there was an incorrigible, dream-chasing optimist, Kearney was it. Despite his record, who else could remain so certain that one day one of his schemes would succeed? Who else would have kept getting up and coming back for more? Who else could match him for maintaining a blind faith in Africa's potential to deliver the fortune he knew was out there just waiting to be discovered?

Kearney, his friends told one another, was in a class of his own on this one, an opinion that would hardly be diminished by the sight of him now, squatting in the dirt miles from anywhere devoid of any means of communication telling a lizard how confident he was of Ryan's imminent arrival.

'Ach,' Kearney reassured his audience, 'nothing to worry about. Your man'll be along any minute. No doubt about it. None at all. He'll have picked up on my mental distress call by now and be well on his way. Anyway, he's surely due for a check on that stash of ostrich bones he's got buried round here somewhere. Can you believe the eejit thinks some gullible tourist with more money than sense will fall for being told they're fossilised dinosaur bones?'

That'll make three of you then, the lizard's face said. If you think you're going to get rescued before your blood scent reaches the man-eaters that rule these parts, you're more of an eejit than Ryan or the tourists he plans to fleece.

'We'll see,' said Kearney's face in reply. 'The telepathic link that's existed between us has never let us down. Well, almost never...' But Kearney didn't want to dwell on that. Doing so might dent his confidence in the link and make him openly admit to wishing he could get a signal on his phone.

Kearney laughed out loud at the thought. 'Phone signal? Around here? I'd be more likely to get wet. The last man to see rain in Tsavo was Noah... probably also the last man to be able to use his phone in these parts. Fockin' Africa.'

It wasn't that Kenya's cell phone network operators hadn't tried. Kearney knew that. It was just that whenever they put up a transmitter in Tsavo it went curiously missing, a bit like the country's landline cable.

Kearney smiled at the thought. Erecting poles to carry the landlines was just inviting trouble. All they did was provide the means of getting to the cable to remove it, its copper core invariably ending up adorning the necks of local tribesmen or in trinkets sold to tourists.

You couldn't blame Kenya's *mwananchi* for this, Kearney muttered to himself. Who could? When you found yourself on the wrong side of the country's obscene rich/poor divide wasn't it only natural to resort to a bit of product recycling? When you saw phone and power lines going over your head to keep the wealthy well-connected and well powered-up – in both senses of the words – wasn't it only natural to want to rebalance the books a bit?

To the armchair socialist in Kearney, the *mwananchi*'s wealth redistribution programme was almost understandable. But what really pissed him off was when those with power and influence got in on the act too, putting the average Kenyan's modest pilfering efforts in the shade.

Well known to everyone – but rarely alluded to in public – was the mass, organised recycling of anything left unguarded in public spaces… the only thing the African could organise in the opinion of some of Kearney's more outspoken acquaintances.

Even close protection was no protection at all while the government paid the police and the judiciary little more than beads. Until they got a proper living wage there was little to stop the determined recycler with influence liberating anything he thought could turn a profit and selling it back to the installer. Kearney knew. He'd been on the wrong end of the recycling scam more times than he cared to count, mostly involving the recycling of his own phone line.

Before the advent of the cell phone the landline was king and, Kearney found himself explaining to the lizard, those who installed the lines the king's tax collectors. Failure to comply with requests for 'something small' to keep you connected meant only one thing – no line, literally. Then the arrival on your doorstep of a grinning phone company representative offering both heartfelt condolences and his personal assistance in reconnecting the line, the one your visitor was invariably holding in one hand, a sizeable scribbled bill for the service in the other.

Kearney and almost everyone he knew on the African continent had had to go through the charade with such regularity you could almost predict when it was coming.

Likewise in the road, railway, power and construction sectors. Nothing was safe from the 'recyclers', especially if they involved projects paid for by foreign governments. So rife was the problem that some development agencies had even declared Africa a lost cause, even some of the saints struggling against overwhelming odds in the humanitarian aid business. One of its top men had openly admitted it to Kearney.

Propped against the bar after a particularly harrowing day, the man had subjected him to a rant so politically incorrect for someone in such a position that Kearney had had to remind himself he hadn't travelled back in time to apartheid South Africa.

'D'you know why the Chinese only employ Chinese to work on their projects here?' the man had slurred at Kearney over his Tusker and whisky chaser. 'It's cos they're the only ones who're not constrained by political niceties. Unlike the rest of us who have to follow the race relations rulebook to the letter, they have no compunction in acting on what the rest of us all know but will only tell each other in private – that if an African can't eat it, drink it, fuck it or steal it, he'll break it.

'I tell you Kal, I'm not the only one who's seriously questioning whether the word "developing" should ever have been applied to Africa. I don't know if you've heard but someone high up in the UN summed it up perfectly the other day. Africa, he said, is a developing country... and always bloody will be.'

Kearney thought that with that, the rant would have run its course.

He was wrong. To the Irishman's wide-eyed surprise, his aid agency drinking partner had then gone on to reveal his true credentials.

'In Africa,' he hissed, 'what's the difference between a tourist and a racist?'

Kearney could only blink.

'About two weeks.'

*   *   *

Having ducked and dived his way across Africa for almost thirty years Kearney thought he was shock-proof. This unbridled summation of the man's deep-seated prejudices convinced him otherwise. If there was one thing that continued to surprise him about the place it was its unlimited capacity for keeping the surprises coming.

In his current circumstances, squatting in the dirt waiting for Ryan to show up, all he could do was hope Africa wasn't in the mood to prove it tonight by dispatching Mwangi to keep him company.

Feared even above hungry lions, Mwangi and the law that went with him was to Kearney what kryptonite is to Superman. Whenever Kearney got close to making a success of anything, up would pop Mwangi to put Murphy's Law in the shade. Under Mwangi's, not only could you be certain of things going wrong that could go wrong but that Mwangi would ensure that someone – or some thing – would materialise from nowhere to make bloody sure they did.

What would it be? What entertaining little event would his nemesis conjure up for him tonight? The thought left Kearney glancing round in trepidation. Whatever it was, if Mwangi revealed himself before the cavalry arrived Kearney knew he was dead meat.

Or, more probably, some very live, very tasty meat.

'Nah,' he told the lizard with as much bravado as he could muster. 'Ryan'll make sure I don't end up as simba's dinner. He'll be along soon enough.'

The lizard looked unconvinced.

''Course he will. You'll see,' Kearney told it sharply. 'Betcha. In the twenty-eight years we've been on this bloody continent, not once has the telepathic link let us down… unless you count that time in Addis when I was being relieved of my wallet in one alleyway while Ryan was being relieved by a Somali hooker in another. Your man still claims he never got the message. But if that was the case why had he already paid for my beer by the time I got to the bar? Most out of character.'

The lizard agreed and Kearney swore he heard it go on to suggest that the communications breakdown might've been down to the telepathic link being in its formative stages at the time. But that might have been the concussion talking.

No matter. The lizard had probably hit the nail on the head. The Addis incident had only been a few weeks into the pair's enforced teaming up as members of an unruly oil crew in Ethiopia's Ogaden desert and the link was still in its developmental phase.

It had taken just one attempt at conversation for Kearney and Ryan to realise they'd need an alternative to the spoken word if their professional relationship was to have any chance of blossoming. From Ireland they both might have been but that's where any commonality stopped, particularly on the communications front.

The issue had come to a head just days after Kearney had quit his Dublin home to take over from the crew's last geologist who'd had to be shipped back to Europe with a nasty case of the clap.

Finding himself stranded miles from camp as a direct result of a misunderstanding with the crew's semi-literate mechanic, it was clear to both that verbal communication between him and the man from Cork should be reserved for emergencies only.

'I thought you said that vehicle was full up,' raged Kearney at Ryan on staggering dehydrated back into camp a day late.

'Oi sed et wear der fool pup,' countered Ryan in a brogue so thick you could have planted bog moss in it.

'Well it wasn't bloody full up, was it?'

'Fool pup yous feckin' eejit! Der pup dat pups der fool. Oi were bout ta feckin' fax 'er wen yous fecked aff interderfeckin' disert!'

The blank look of bemusement spreading across Kearney's face as Ryan gave him both incomprehensible barrels brought help from an unlikely source. The mechanic's grinning Somali assistant suddenly found himself elevated to camp translator-in-chief.

'Mr Lion tell fool pump, no fol ap,' he managed in response to Kearney's pleading look in his direction, the irony of an African having to interpret for two men from the same European country not escaping him for a moment.

'What?'

'Fool pump. He fixing.'

Kearney's eyes went from one man to the other and back again before enlightenment finally dawned. Fool pump…? Fool pump…? Kerrrist! FUEL pump!

'Jayzus! Why didn't you fockin' say so when I asked if she was ready to go?'

'Ois feckin' ded. Yous feckin' dafersomten'?'

Kearney thought about replying but then thought better of it. He knew when he was beaten… and when an alternative plan of action was needed. Since he was incapable of, as Ryan put it, 'lisnin' in der roit agsent', it was clearly best if words were reserved for last resort.

The end result had been a rapidly-developed, highly individual form of Irish sign language to augment verbal communication until a reliable telepathic link had been established – a system of grunts, shrugs and finger jabbing that had the rest of the crew looking on in belly-holding mirth, the Americans in particular.

How, they asked, was it possible for two men from a country no bigger than a leprechaun's testicle not to understand what the other was saying?

While the invective contained in Ryan's spittle-flecked gattling gun response just served to add fuel to the fire of collective crew amusement, Kearney stood aloof from the proceedings smiling inwardly. Unlike the rest of the crew, now that he and Ryan 'understood' one another so-to-speak, he could now set off in one of the vehicles Ryan had been working on with some degree of confidence of getting back.

To the rest of the crew, Kearney's self-assurance just served as an opportunity to lay bets. But as the weeks went by, those wagering on the need to mount a search party were to be disappointed. Not only did Kearney keep bringing his vehicle home but the pair's signing performances began waning in direct proportion to the level of telepathic understanding that had begun to take over. An understanding so twin-like that, by the time their contracts were up, they'd not only dispensed with the signing system altogether but had somehow managed to cement their relationship with a joint silent pledge. Until their fortunes in Africa were made, both Ireland and its peat bogs would just have to get by without them.

* * *

That had been more than a quarter of a century ago and still the only things they had to show for their endeavours were the vehicle that had ferried them the length and breadth of the continent, a tool kit that was the envy of every African mechanic and a string of horror stories to test the nerve of Alfred Hitchcock himself.

Somehow the Millennium Falcon – a 1990 V8 Landrover just two years old when they'd taken it in lieu of their leaving bonuses and named after Han Solo's fleet-beating craft in Star Wars on the grounds that it was the fastest thing in this particular universe – had survived a dunking in the crocodile-infested Zambezi, a concerted rhino attack in the Serengeti, a falling monster tree in Malawi, the maulings of any number of local mechanics trying to help and – the one that made the pair shiver most – a plunge into a six-foot deep snake-filled pit concealed in some of the densest, most uninviting jungle along the Congo river.

The story of how they got the Falcon out of that had kept the pair in dinners for weeks and one day, Kearney vowed, he'd write it all down, make himself that promised fortune and retire to running a bar and a book at the Galway races.

'One day, one day,' he told the lizard which shrugged, rolled its eyes and turned its attention to more likely eventualities. A juicy beetle had just blundered its way on to his rock.

'Bastard,' said Kearney. 'I'll show you. I WILL write a book. I fockin' will. Then you'll be sorry. While I'm living the life of Reilly with a best seller and a film deal to my name, you'll still be chasing fockin' beetles.'

'Go on then,' said the lizard. 'Prove it.'

'I fockin' will,' said Kearney. 'Starting right now.'

'You've got nothing to write with.'

'I'll do it in my head.'

'Fraud.'

'Beetle murderer.'

'Fraud.'

'Fock off, lizard.'

Actually, Kearney thought, now really might be a good time to start. The mental fog was at last beginning to lift and he didn't have much else to do except wait for fate to take its course. He could use the time to map out the storyline.

Where, though, to start? There was enough material to fill Wikipedia. And how to make it different to all the other foreigner-in-Africa books gathering dust on Waterstone's shelves? There was only one way his was going to make the bestseller lists. It had to be different. It had to have an angle. It had to be unique.

'Fraud,' said the lizard.

'Fock off,' said Kearney. 'I'm doing it.'

'No you're not,' said the lizard.

'I am.'

'You're not.'

'What makes you so sure?'

'You're talking to a fockin' lizard.'

chapter five

Kearney did his best to concentrate. But every time he glimpsed of a way of making his book different, his current predicament and the irony of how he came to be in it intervened.

Not six weeks earlier he'd found himself in almost the exact same situation in almost the exact same spot for almost the exact same reason. Then, as now, his plight could be traced directly back to having to resort to shopping for replacement car parts in the store of one of the dodgiest dealers in the dodgiest part of Nairobi's dodgy car part heartland, something he'd vowed he'd never do again but of course had.

Potless as usual but knowing the Falcon's original tie rod ends – two small but vital parts of the steering mechanism that effectively held the driver's life in their hands – were long past their kill-by date, Kearney had had no option but to seek out a pair of Chinese-made knock-off replacements.

As Kearney handed over a wad of shilling bills for the pair, he knew he'd regret it. The penalty for not fitting genuine parts, tie rod ends in particular, was the cold sweat of fear every time your vehicle got above Thomson's gazelle speed.

But what choice did he have? Another failed venture – this time involving a raggedy Swahili reggae band who'd grinned with delight on being introduced to their new, Kearney-funded, band equipment before promptly disappearing with it into the bush – had left him without the funds to cover his rent, let alone the purchase of car parts you could trust.

When one of the tie rod ends inevitably crumbled to dust a couple of months later, then as now, he'd been lucky to come out of that one alive.

Escaping to Mombasa from a romantic interlude he'd rather not have happened, Kearney gasped in horror as the Falcon veered out of control across the barrier-less Nairobi/Mombasa highway ending up at a rakish angle in a roadside trench left by a Chinese road gang some twenty miles north of the ravine where the Falcon now lay.

When that tie rod end snapped, Kearney found himself clinging to a useless steering wheel as the Landrover slewed drunkenly into the path of a monster truck bearing down on him like a rogue bull elephant blinded by lust and territorial fury.

It could have been carnage but fate decided otherwise. Just one mile an hour faster and the truck would've added the Falcon to the crust of insects barbequing nicely on its bull bar.

Air brakes and buffalo horns screaming, the truck's dinner plate-eyed driver had managed to rein his charge in just enough to prevent a full-on wipe-out but not enough to avoid clipping the Falcon's rear end and send it spinning into the trench.

Then, as now, Kearney had had to wait for the world, his mind and his legs to stop gyrating before he could dismount his battered steed and focus on what to do next.

With no one stopping to help – carjacking paranoia had long since put a stop to good Samaritan deeds on Kenya's roads – Kearney knew he was on his own. But at least that time he was within cell phone signal range and Ryan wasn't far away looking after the safari vehicles at Bushwacker Camp.

When he'd stopped laughing, Ryan had mobilised the camp's breakdown truck and hauled the remains of the Falcon back to Bushwacker's, a more rudimentary version of Kenya's more celebrated safari lodges and named in honour of a particularly sneaky pride of local lions that took no shit from anyone stupid enough to get out of their vehicle to admire the view.

'Jayzus,' said Ryan, 'gonna tek som fexin' dat iz,' and had had to dig deep to find the funds Kearney lacked to buy his countryman a second class train ticket to Nairobi to shop for the necessary parts.

As he squatted in the dirt staring down at the Falcon's upended form staring forlornly back at him from the dried-up riverbed, it occurred to Kearney that that was when the sequence of events leading to his current predicament had started. Or, more accurately, the moment he'd first handed over money for Chinese junk.

Had he had the funds for genuine parts in the first place it was unlikely he'd have ended up in the ditch near Bushwacker's and therefore not on the train, a trip that'd proved to be the inspiration for a money-making scheme that, until Kearney's most recent excursion into the ravine, had put both him and Ryan within touching distance of the riches that'd evaded them for so long.

* * *

Shackled to a handrail in the train conductor's compartment, Kearney had had an epiphany.

'My GOD!' he'd exclaimed to himself. 'That's it! Why the fock didn't I think of it before?' Probably, he thought, because his mind hadn't been treated to a good old-fashioned Kenya Railways jolting for many a year.

No one took the clapped-out, deathtrap trains these days if they could help it. But that, thought Kearney, might have been where he'd been missing out. Although the jolting had left him facing the prospect of a lengthy interview with the Kenya police, the upside was that without it the idea might never have occurred.

Boarding the clunking night-time loco hulk that had for years been regularly falling off the Mombasa/Nairobi line, Kearney had found himself groping in the dark in more ways than one.

First it was to the right carriage on the pitch black platform of Voi station, Bushwacker's closest stop. Then it was to his compartment along the lightless carriage corridor. Finally it was to the private parts of a fellow passenger as the train lurched to a violent shuddering halt in the middle of nowhere.

Thrown off balance, Kearney had grabbed the first thing that had come to hand and, via the conductor's compartment, the screams of the thing's owner had carried all the way to Nairobi where the Kenya police had leapt indolently into action.

Kearney never did make it to his bunk that night. Instead, chained to the handrail, he spent the rest of the twenty lurching hour journey putting flesh on the bones of a fortune-making plan that this time, he was utterly convinced, was foolproof.

As he sat wondering how to explain himself to the police he'd had a sudden blinding flash of inspiration. Not only did he, Ryan and Kenya Railways share the same initials but all three had two other things in common. All were equally in need of funds and all needed them equally urgently.

But there, it occurred to Kearney, all commonality stopped. Unlike Kearney and Ryan, it looked like KR's prayer had been answered. A not-inconsiderable amount of Chinese money had been earmarked to modernise the railway's lines and rolling stock and bring the train service properly into the twenty-first century.

'Jaysus,' thought Kearney. 'If a company as inept and corrupt as Kenya Railways can pick China's pockets, why not Ryan and me?' But how?

Thirty-five KR jolts later he had it, and as the eureka smile of enlightenment lit up Kearney's face another thing of equal certainty spread through his mind. If he didn't wipe the smile off his face before the train pulled into Nairobi station he'd have some difficulty convincing the police they hadn't, as they thought, finally nabbed the infamous, highly elusive and equally highly sought-after Mombasa Express groper.

chapter six

The oil exploration crew Kearney and Ryan joined in 1989 was American-run. These days they'd more likely be working for the Chinese. Or rather, they wouldn't. All Chinese-run companies operating in Africa were exclusively Chinese-staffed save for the manual labour, African almost to a man.

Although the yanks were still around, they were heavily out-gunned by Chinese operations all thanks to the collapse of the Soviet Union and, Kearney and Ryan dared to venture, Ireland's attempt to colonise Africa.

To their immense vexation, the arrival of Kearney and Ryan in Africa never made the Irish or even the local press. At the time, both were taken up with something considered of somewhat greater significance.

With impeccable timing, the pair arrived on site the very day the Berlin wall came down and Africa stopped being of such strategic importance to the USA. No longer did Washington have to prop up spurious regimes to keep the Commies out and suddenly covertly US government-sponsored operations like the one to which Kearney and Ryan were attached saw their CIA colour code pale from a bright crimson to a sort of washed-out pastel magnolia.

When it became obvious to all on the crew that someone somewhere had cut their operational funding, a collective sigh of exasperation ran through the camp. Big mistake, everyone agreed. This, after all, was Ethiopia, the place where an earlier

US exploration crew had had to scurry out the back door when the Soviet-backed Marxist maniac Haile Mariam Mengistu overthrew Emperor Haile Selassie in 1974.

Even though the post-Mengistu regime was proving more accommodating than its predecessor, inviting the US company back in to pick up where it'd left off, you didn't need a Deep Thought computer to work out that the pendulum could swing again at any moment.

It wasn't Russia the US had to worry about this time. Now it was communist China. Beijing was looking for friends in Africa and unless the US showed a little more enthusiasm in helping Ethiopia join the ranks of the world's oil producers, Addis Ababa would look elsewhere for help and the obvious direction was to the East.

Which is exactly what happened. Without the Soviet Union around, the US company remobilised with all the urgency of a three-toed sloth and when the Ethiopian government realised its guest was doing no more than go through the motions using the same rusting equipment it'd abandoned two decades earlier, there was only ever going to be one outcome. The Ogaden desert concession was withdrawn from the US company and handed to the Chinese.

Although that was well after Kearney and Ryan had jumped ship taking the Millennium Falcon with them, the signs were there long before, prompting one African business commentator to dub the US exploratory effort 'a dribs and drabs operation limping along at the pace of a homeless drunk's move towards the pub door at chucking out time.'

It was a piece of symbolism that appealed to the two Irishmen despite the dribs and drabs description which, as their own chucking out time loomed one night, had been viewed in a more personal light than had been intended.

'Dribs and drabs is it,' grumbled Kearney into his beer. 'Which one's which d'you think? You wanna be Mr Drib or Mr Drab?' he asked Ryan.

'Oi'll tek Drib,' slurred Ryan. 'Notin' drab 'bout me.'

Kearney was minded to agree. In fact he was minded to agree with anything Ryan said at such times lest his countryman forget for a moment that they were countrymen.

''n oi'll tell yous anudder ting,' continued the man from Cork, eyes gleaming with alcoholic enlightenment, 'dees peepl don't know what dey've got in der pair of us two. If dey did, dey wudn't be goin' callin' us names. Dey'd be rollin' out der red feckin' carpet!'

'Right. How, exactly?'

'Jayzus! Yous need me ter feckin' explain it to yous? A man o' feckin' letters loike yersel'!'

'Humour me,' said Kearney hoping that hadn't come across like something his old university tutor might have said when talking down to mere mortals.

'Humour yous? Humour yous? Oi'll feckin' humour yous, yous feckin' bollock-brained bog trotter! How's dis fer feckin' humour? Der feckin' Choi-feckin'-nees wudn't have started sniffin' round Africa if it wasn't for the feckin' Oirish, yous and mees in 'ticular, 'n dat's a fact. How's dat fer feckin' humour?' And with that Ryan nodded with satisfaction, drew the figure 'one' in the air with his index finger and turned his attention back to his bottle considering further explanation unnecessary.

Kearney looked silently at his own as if waiting for it to take pity on him and put him out of his misery. When it didn't, he was just about to hold up a finger of his own and politely request a re-run when Ryan pre-empted him.

'Dem feckin' Choinees. Yous can just imagine dem squarkin' amongst demselves, can't ye? "Jayzus", dey'd have bin frettin', "der feckin' Oirish are in Africa! If we don't get in quick der'll be notin' feckin' left!'"

* * *

Over subsequent years Ryan's China-in-Africa-because-of-the-Irish theory had become the stuff of legend, the continent's European expatriate community slapping their thighs every time the story was told.

To their credit, neither Kearney nor Ryan ever took umbrage when it was recounted in their presence. They simply reacted with looks of pantomime pouting indignation, a knowing smile and a tap on the nose.

Ever, that is, except once – the time one smarmy American academic actually made a serious attempt to rubbish the theory. On that occasion, at a ritzy Nairobi drinks party the pair had been mistakenly invited to long after they'd done a runner from Ethiopia, the American had not only escaped close contact with the punch bowl but, in trying to disprove the theory, only succeeded in proving a second – that wit inhibitors and attention deficit accentuators are implanted in Americans at birth.

At first the pair thought the man was entering into the spirit of things by expounding his view that China's interest in Africa had more to do with tying the continent up in silk ribbon than to the opening of Guinness breweries from Cairo to Cape Town. The thought lasted all of a second, dissipating rapidly on the astonishing discovery that the man actually thought they were being serious.

'Whilst not seeking to downplay Ireland's involvement in prompting China to move in on Africa,' the academic sniffily informed them as their grins started turning to gawps of amazement, 'I think you'll find that China's arrival here can be directly traced to the foreign influence vacuum that had developed across the continent once the threat of Soviet expansionism no longer had to be countered by the West.

'To the Chinese elite,' he said with a perfect white crocodile smile and a look of immense self-satisfaction on his smug, pointy-bearded face at having come up with the analogy, 'Africa is to China what the online banking novice is to the computer hacker – an easy mugging victim just begging to be fleeced. And once it'd chosen its victim it didn't take China long to start dispatching shiploads of workers to carry out the operation.

'The first step,' he went indefatigably on as if imparting privileged information to two yokels accorded the honour of a moment of his time, 'was to win Africa's confidence through a soft power charm offensive offering hospitals, roads, sports stadiums and the like in return for, well, not very much. All it was asking was that the target government switch its diplomatic ties – if it hadn't done so already – from the renegade Taiwan to the People's Republic of China... and the odd mining concession.'

Mistaking the pair's gawping mouths for rapt attention, the man blustered superciliously on in the self-assured assumption that Kearney and Ryan were hanging on every word.

'As is plain to anyone who's studied the subject,' he continued as Kearney telepathically imposed a nose-bloodying restraining order on Ryan, 'most African governments have been only too willing to oblige. Switching allegiances is, after all, but a scrap of paper and every signature to it carries the promise of a sizeable pot of corrupt gold for those holding power of attorney over the signing country.'

As his 'educator' paused for a sip of his drink, a thin-lipped Kearney decided this was too good an opportunity to miss.

'Bejaysus, dat's amazin' ain't it?' he said in his broadest bog trotting brogue with a wink at Ryan. 'Ter tink dat we've been wrong all dis time. So it wasn't Dublin's plan to send in Saint Patrick to clear Africa o' snakes and plant the continent wid potaters. All der toime it wuz Choina's intention to fill Africa wid computer hackers. Is dat what yous sayin'?'

For a moment Kearney thought the man's perfect plastic smile was going to crack but all it did was freeze on his smarmy patronising face. Just long enough for Kearney to fix him with a glittering, semi-drunk eye and transmit the message through his week-in-the-bush-without-access-to-hot-water stubble that if the man wanted to walk from the gathering with both teeth and face intact he might like to consider reviewing how he talked to people at parties.

'And while we're on the subject of clearing things up,' Kearney added in his own accent to press the message home, 'I wonder if you'd be good enough to confirm something else for me. Is it true that the word "gullible" has been deleted from American dictionaries?'

* * *

It wasn't that Kearney wasn't interested in what the pompous prick had to say. It was that the prick was getting an obscene amount of money for proselytising to a bunch of nose-picking students what it had taken Kearney and Ryan almost three decades to learn through bitter, virtually unpaid experience and he rather took exception to having it relayed back to him by a prime example of strutting puffed-up self-importance.

Fortunately for the American, the look in Kearney's eye had not gone unnoticed by another guest who, unlike the American, did possess a sense of humour. Out of the shadows stepped a willowy, self-assured African woman in a cream business suit who'd stood aloof from the exchange smiling as she watched Kearney's face grow a shade darker with every condescending word of the American's sanctimonious homily.

Stepping in to quell what was looking like descending into a fracas worthy of a piece in the Kenya *Daily Nation*'s gossip columns, the woman neatly punctured the balloon of enmity with one well-timed intervention.

'I hope you don't mind me butting in, but I for one would welcome Saint Patrick's arrival in Africa,' she said with a broad grin in the direction of both adversaries. 'I know it's not ecologically *de rigueur* to say so these days but I can't abide snakes and the sooner Dublin dispatches Ireland's patron saint to rid the African continent of them the better in my opinion.

'Not sure about the potatoes though. Not enough rain you see and the soil might not be to their liking. Tried planting them on my *shamba* once. Had about as much success as the Chinese are having with their rice, er, paddies – no offence.'

'None taken,' said Kearney, relaxing on finally finding there was someone else in the universe on his own wavelength. 'Except the name's not Paddy,' he said. 'It's Kearney. Anthony Kearney. People call me Kal... and this is Ryan'

'Beatrice Kinyui,' said the woman holding out her hand to Kearney, 'a lowly operative in the hive of the administration here which is why people call me Bee.'

'Professor Aloysius S. Pratt the third from Stanford,' said the smarmy American edging between Kearney and the woman and holding out a limp-wristed collection of expensively-manicured digits. 'People call me Professor.'

Ryan just stood there clenching and unclenching his fists and hoping Professor Pratt – a more perfect name for such a gombeen gobshite he could scarcely imagine – would give him the chance to use them by going on to rubbish one of his other pet theories... that the arrival of the Chinese in Africa was directly responsible for the complete, continent-wide, absence of tigers.

If Pratt thought of doing so, he had second thoughts. Instead, he turned his oily attention fully on the newcomer, someone he clearly viewed as having the power to make life difficult for critics of Kenya government policy – especially ones suspected of trying to undermine Kenya's burgeoning relationship with China.

If there was a more obvious attempt to dig one's self out of a hole and in the process make it deeper, none of the other three had witnessed it. All Pratt achieved through diverting the subject matter to Chinese rice growing was to prompt the exchange of a series of eye-rolling looks between the members of his new, larger, audience.

'Ah. Yes. Rice,' he mumbled into his drink. 'Think I once read a paper on the problems of growing it in Africa. Pests, wasn't it?'

'Nutrients,' corrected Kinyui matter-of-factly transmitting the first of the looks in Kearney's direction.

'Nutrients? Right. Yeees. Now I come to think of it… yes, nutrients. Surprising really, not being able to grow rice in soil that has so much wealth in it. I mean, all those rare earths the Chinese find so enticing. Must be stuffed full of nutrients. Perhaps it's because they're so rare, eh?'

This time the looks exchanged were ones of pity.

'I think, PROFESSOR, that you'll find that rare earth is just a name,' interjected Kearney the geologist. 'It's what they call certain minerals which are vital in the production of some electronic components.'

'Maybe that's what you call them your side of the pond, son,' countered Pratt defensively. 'Stateside we call things what they are. If it's an earth and it's rare, it's a rare earth.

'Anyhow, that doesn't solve the problem of nutrient deficiency,' the professor blundered on. 'You'd have thought the Chinese would have checked that out before they planted, eh? Sounds like a case of leaping without looking to me. Probably because they're the new boys in the hood. If they'd talked to old Uncle Sam first we might have been able to put 'em straight.'

'Actually they're not the new boys in the 'hood' as you put it,' said Kinyui. 'They've had trade links with Africa stretching back centuries.'

Professor Pratt and the other two blinked at her.

'Seriously. There's a lot of evidence that the Chinese arrived on our shores well before the Arabs or the Europeans. I've been on a Chinese language course at the local Confucius Institute lately and that's one of the first things the course instructor dwelt on. The links apparently go back to the second century BC, blossoming in the Ming dynasty when China's famous navigator Zheng He arrived on Kenya's own shores to cement a China/Africa trade relationship.'

'Well, ma'am,' blustered the professor, 'while I've no wish to doubt the veracity of your words, would it not be in the interests of scientific enquiry to question the source of the information?'

'Professor Pratt,' countered Kinyui sharply, 'if you're referring to the reliability of information pertaining to China as supplied by an institute funded by the Chinese government, let me assure you that that aspect has not escaped my attention. It may interest you to know that not everyone attending Confucius Institute courses allows their heads to be filled with information they haven't subsequently checked.'

'Sincere apologies ma'am. I wasn't trying to infer…'

'No. I'm sure you weren't, Professor,' Kinyui smiled sweetly back.

The awkward silence that ensued was broken by an unlikely source. Ryan piped up for the first time to ask Kearney if he'd heard that right.

'Wod's she feckin' sayin'? Dat der feckin' Choi-feckin'-nees discovered feckin' Africa afor der feckin' woyt man? If dat's wot de auld tert is sayin' yous kin tell her she's tarkin' outer her feckin' erse.'

'Sorry, Mr Ryan. Not sure…'

'He's saying that if that's the case,' said Kearney with a sharp glance in Ryan's direction, 'could he a-a-sk you if the course threw up any other interesting revelations.'

'Oh. Right. Well, yes it did as it happens.'

While Kinyui regurgitated some of the figures she'd had thrust upon her by her Chinese course instructor – over two and a half thousand Chinese companies now in Africa helping take Sino-African trade to well over two hundred billion dollars, well over twice the US/Africa trade figure and forecast to double within a couple of decades – Kearney's mind had slipped away, off on a quick safari of its own. You didn't need a representative of Kenya's administration or a Chinese government flunky to tell you how much the Africa/China relationship had grown in the space of just a few years. You could read all about it in *The Economist*, something Kearney did whenever he could afford the haughty, over-priced magazine.

What hadn't been in the *Economist* though – and most certainly wouldn't have been in the Chinese flunky's presentation – was the real reason the relationship had been forged… to reintroduce slavery into Africa.

Despite China's vehement refutation of the charge, Kearney knew from his own contact with Africans that the official Chinese line – the one about China's primary goal being to do what Africa's former colonial masters had never done and bring Africa out of poverty via the trade route – was so much shuch water.

Africans Kearney knew who'd taken the Chinese shilling for working on their construction and mining projects got just that, a shilling. The lack of enforceable minimum wage laws Africa-wide meant the Chinese could get away with paying Africans what they liked and treat them like dogs into the bargain.

To say that there was no love lost between the African labour force and the Chinese was like saying there was no love lost between Africans and the mosquito. 'Both are out to suck your blood,' grizzled one Kenyan friend to Kearney. 'The only difference is that there are ways to treat a mosquito's diseases. None if you contract Chineses.'

The feeling was said to be mutual. There was even a story doing the rounds that the Chinese took their own towels to hotels in Africa in case the ones provided had previously been used by Africans. And one drunk Chinese had even told him quite openly that Chinese respect for Africans registered zero. 'If they don't respect themselves,' the man had said, 'why should we?'

The comment left Kearney feeling torn. On the one hand, having seen with his own eyes how Africans treated one another, he had some sympathy with the viewpoint. On the other, coming from a country that'd been on the receiving end of colonialism itself, he couldn't help but empathise with the African condition.

All of which had left him in something of a quandary when listening to the American prick. As much as Kearney hated the idea of agreeing with him, he was undoubtedly spot-on with his appraisal of China's real reason for taking Africa under its wing. The idea, clear to anyone who hadn't been blinded by the bling with which China was flooding Africa, was to colonise the continent economically, starting with what everyone hereabouts called China's sports stadium diplomacy policy.

Just like Africa's former colonialists, Beijing came offering baubles. This time, though, the baubles weren't intended as sweeteners to win power and influence. China had a more straightforward offer. You get a bunch of sports stadiums, hospitals, roads, railways and glittering new public buildings like the Chinese-built African Union HQ in Addis Ababa, they said, and we get a blank cheque to plunder the continent's barely-touched mineral resources.

The number of African tyrant's spurning China's advances could be counted on the noses of Africa's tiger population. Which was hardly surprising since the tyrants were doing very nicely out of it and, into the bargain, could tell the people they ruled with almost utmost sincerity that the Africa/China conjoining was a win-win relationship.

The Chinese-inspired phrase was especially relevant when it came to the way the tyrants ruled their people. Of all the wins won, top of the pile was China's pledge not to interfere in African politics. All it wanted was a healthy trade relationship. And anyway, Beijing said, it had no right lecturing Africa on the way it conducted its affairs.

To Kearney, of all China's pronunciations, for candour this last stood head and shoulders above the rest. With a human rights record to equal the worst excesses of any African potentate, had the slapping of wrists been part of the deal both pot and kettle would rapidly have become worn-out commentator allusions.

While Kearney's feelings for the Chinese echoed those of his African mates, this degree of candour left him torn again. He couldn't help but harbour a grudging respect for the way the Chinese did business in Africa. At least they were honest – more or less – about why they were there which was a lot more than could be said of the continent's former colonisers, one of which his own country had had a bit of local difficulty with.

Just as it had with the Irish, the olive branch Africa's biggest coloniser Britain carried when arriving on African shores had a cynical secondary purpose – to camouflage the heavy artillery following up behind.

'We're here to do good,' Africa's smiling eighteenth and nineteenth century visitors had insisted, only revealing the crocodile behind the smile when Africa dropped its guard. The continent's only attraction lay in whatever could be plundered and repatriated to Britain, France, Spain, Portugal, Belgium, the Netherlands, Germany and the New World, animal as well as vegetable and mineral.

'African animism is an affront to the sensibilities of any right-thinking, God-fearing man and needs to be eradicated,' went the colonisers' battle cry of self-righteous indignation. 'The African has to be saved from himself,' they told one another, almost meaning it.

The message to Africa's indigenous inhabitants was slightly different. 'A decent education and a shirt for your back awaits if you'll just don these designer chains and board our luxury cruise liners for an all-expenses-paid trip to the land of milk and honey.'

Somehow, the information that the education would be taking place in the fields of the American South where they'd first have to grow the cotton to make the shirts for their backs got lost in translation.

Until China's late twentieth century arrival, only the Arabs had been honest about why they were there.

'So what's the problem?' they'd said. 'Slavery is as old as the scriptures and just as unquestioned where we're from. And since there's a whole continent of human sub-species on our doorstep waiting to be taken advantage of it'd be folly not to make use of it.'

All of which set Kearney thinking. If it was true what Beatrice Kinyui had been saying about China's long history with Africa, why hadn't they arrived at exactly the same conclusion when first setting serious foot on African shores in the fifteenth century?

It was a question that was to linger long after the ritzy drinks party, Kearney only receiving an answer sometime after he and the woman from the ministry had become somewhat better acquainted in the back of the Millennium Falcon.

45

chapter seven

Xi Ren would have been able to understand the severity of his sentence had an intention to support the Tiananmen demonstrators been anywhere near the front of his mind.

But nothing had been further from it. While half the student population of Beijing was getting exercised about democracy, the only thing concerning Xi was rocks. Or more precisely, books about rocks.

His mistake, as he was to find out, was choosing that day of all days to collect a reference work for his geology course from a bookshop in the very street the army chose to corral those fleeing the brutality of the crackdown.

Indistinguishable from the demonstrators, Xi's own protests of being nothing to do with it went unheard by both the security forces and the magistrates and, in thirty seconds flat, he'd been found guilty of subversion and sentenced to an unlimited term of public servitude. The magistrates weren't joking. China's judicial system really was based on 'leniency for those who confess, severity for those who deny their crime'.

Had they known how sticking so rigidly to this guiding principle was to rebound on them, the magistrates might have thought twice before condemning Xi to a life of penal misery, wrecking all his dreams in the process. Rather than 'encouraging' the miscreant to mend his subversive ways, all the sentence did was turn a hitherto model citizen into the very thing the state feared most. Xi had become the human equivalent of a death watch beetle patiently waiting its chance to emerge from suspended animation and start eating at the system's fabric from within.

Before his court case, Xi had never had cause to question or oppose the Chinese state. It seemed to be treating him well enough. It had housed him, fed him and kept him warm in his youth and had, until now, provided him with all the education he needed to fulfil his dream of helping extend the country's geological knowledge base. In fact, from what he'd heard of the West and its obsession with religious superstition – denying the existence of a geological timeframe that was staring them squarely in the face – he might even go so far as to describe himself as a system devotee.

But that was before he discovered just how vindictive, vengeful and utterly bereft of feeling it could be.

That discovery came the day the place selected for Xi to do his public service was revealed to him.

'Oh, ha bloody ha,' he'd yelled through the soup of dust and smog perpetually blotting out the sun in Shanxi province, China's foremost coal producing region. 'Very bloody funny.'

How, he wondered, could those with the power of life over death have managed not to snigger on informing Xi he was being sent to a region where his geological training would be of immense benefit to the country.

As appreciative as he was of the joke, what Xi didn't know was that it was only half told. Only on stepping off the train at the coalfield was he to be let in on the rest. The system had decided that the best use of Xi's geology skills would be in doing something about as far removed from those skills as it was possible to get.

No sooner had Xi left the train than he found himself on the summit of a vast coal mountain armed with a mighty hammer and the knowledge that here in the coalfield he was completely expendable. If the work didn't kill him, one slip on the miniscule platform he was teetering on most certainly would. Xi had been allocated the job of bucket basher, the man responsible for ensuring nothing remained in the coal conveyor belt buckets as they dumped their loads on to the unstable mountain groaning and creaking below Xi's poorly-shod feet.

It hadn't taken Xi long to understand why the job was specially reserved for miscreants, particularly those convicted of subversion. The combination of the monstrous coal-ferrying machinery in perpetual motion above his head coupled with the equally mobile scree of coal beneath him made this the most dangerous job in the coal industry. More life-threatening even than mining the stuff, an occupation which even the carefully manicured official figures showed left hundreds of miners' wives widowed each year.

As Xi struggled to maintain his balance on the platform and deliver ringing blows to the buckets with his hammer, a thought occurred. This must be why so many people were convicted on spurious evidence every year in China. If the state-run coal industry couldn't pay people enough to take the job, they'd have to 'recruit' them so-to-speak. The average lifespan of a bucket basher couldn't be much longer than a lump of coal in a furnace and the state would need a regular supply of expendables to fill the boots of those whose luck had run out.

As the thought struck, Xi was suddenly consumed with another. How many of his predecessors still lay unrecovered in the coal mountain beneath him, swallowed up and sinking into the black mass, their screams going unheard over the din of the machinery above? The thought of that death made him shiver. Not just with fear but with rage.

Before his own 'recruitment' to the coalfields, the Communist Party dogma of the individual being subordinate to the state was little more than that to the young student. He'd never felt particularly subordinated. What intrusion into his life he'd experienced he just took as standard operating procedure. When the state said it knew best, he'd just taken it as fact and got on with his life.

But that was before the epiphany the state itself had delivered to his door. His education, he realised, was the result of the deaths of god-knew how many men, sacrificed on the altar of the state juggernaut so it could keep on rolling over their dead bodies.

The epiphany had Xi screaming at the buckets, attacking them with all his might. To the young man newly-educated in real, ungilded statecraft, each one represented a member of the Chinese Communist Party politburo, the real enemies of the state, and every one of them needed to be smashed. It was the only way to put an end to this madness.

While Xi worked off his fury on the buckets, the men who ran the machinery stood at the base of the mountain looking up at him, occasionally glancing at their watches.

Each had picked three times – how long it'd be before the new man's anger got the better of him and he started taking it out on the buckets, how long he could last before he broke down and wept, and how long it'd be before he realised they were placing bets on him and started screaming vile oaths down the mountainside.

'You fucking brain-dead bastards!' yelled Xi as his strength began to ebb and he saw money changing hands. 'Can't you see what's fucking going on here? You're as dehumanised as the autocrats who're pulling your brainless strings.'

His unheard outburst spent, Xi sank to his knees and wept. But only until he saw a second and then a third money-changing transaction in progress. It was the motivation he needed to haul himself back to his feet with a new resolve.

There'd be no more profiting from his misfortune, he'd decided. If they were also placing bets on how long he'd last before joining those who'd gone before him into their mass, pitch black grave they were going to be disappointed. That, he'd resolved, was not going to happen – if only for the satisfaction of beating those who held his well-being in their filthy hands at their own inhuman game.

* * *

To Xi's amazement, his resilience was rewarded not only with his life but with two surprising bonuses. Having withstood three full months of this torture they brought him down and handed him the first – the final pot which, thanks to his resolve and a bit of guile, had gone unclaimed. He was right. They had had money on whether the job would kill him.

What he didn't know though was that the bucket-bashing job wasn't strictly necessary. Thanks to advances made in coal mining technology, these days it was just a test. One designed by those who decided the fate of miscreants to break and then re-make them… if they survived.

The fact that Xi had and that he'd used his wits to do so, fashioning a harness out of an old piece of conveyor belt to stop him plunging to his death if he ever slipped or passed out, won him the grudging respect of all who'd witnessed him transforming from a scrawny callow youth into a full-grown, muscle-bound man.

To his controllers' surprise, that respect was met not with gratitude but with sullen, silent indifference. Although they didn't know it, part of their plan had succeeded. While they hadn't broken Xi, they had re-made him. Without knowing it, they'd produced a volcano shrouded in mist.

Three months of hard labour in almost total isolation in all weathers had given Xi time to look into the minds of his jailers and work out a strategy for bringing them and the system they served to book. In that time, Xi had progressed steadily from mindless, incandescent rage to pensive, seething indignation and ultimately to a state of calm, calculated planning. What the state had produced was a man resolved to keep his fury hidden until the opportunity arose to erupt and smother the system under a seething lava flow of white hot retribution.

Xi's indifference was taken in just the way he hoped – as proof of a spirit broken. But if he expected his controllers to leave it at that and release him back to his pre-custodial life he was to be disappointed. The breaking of the miscreant's spirit, it was soon to become clear, was but the first of many stages of the rehabilitation process.

The second came in the form of his second bonus. One day of rest later, he was taken to the one place he'd never expected to see. After finding himself condemned to the top of the coal mountain, a job in the core sample logging office seemed about as conceivable as a full pardon.

But as if the state was determined to keep the surprises coming that's exactly where Xi found himself. The chief sample logger's assistant had been seriously injured in a drilling accident and the department needed a replacement fast.

Even though his detention had deprived Xi of taking his final exams, he had all the training necessary to qualify him for the position and the departmental chief had breathed a sigh of relief on being informed by the custodial authorities that, despite their better judgement, they could let him have Xi for as long as the state could spare him.

Seven years as it turned out. Costing nothing to employ save for his food and lodging, the chief was only too glad to train Xi into the job and keep him for as long as he could. The pittance Xi was supposed to be getting was keeping the chief's family in rather more comfort than one salary alone could sustain.

In all that time Xi said not one word to rock the boat. His boss could keep his money. Complaining about it wasn't in Xi's grand plan. Central to it was keeping his nose clean, his mouth shut and his ear to the ground listening for signs that his jailers were convinced he'd been fully rehabilitated.

Only when sure they felt confident they'd done their job of transforming him from radical subversive enemy of the state into obedient model of state compliancy would they discover what they'd really created – a state-manufactured composite of Winston Smith, Papillon and the Count of Monte Cristo.

chapter eight

Staring at the fossil in the light of his Kenya badlands campfire, Xi wondered where he'd gone wrong. He'd played all his cards right yet full rehabilitation still eluded him.

Not for the first time on this expedition he ran through it in his head. Could it really be that one little slip he'd made on being informed that his time was up at the core sample logging office? Could his exclamation really have been deemed proof of his underlying failure to conform?

All he'd done when told that the quality of his coal reserve reports qualified him for a placement at China's state news agency was to remind his handlers of his technical expertise. Nothing more.

But seeing them pause, look at one another then make a careful note of his 'But I'm a geologist…' response to their announcement had, he had to confess, sent a ripple of anxiety down his spine. He'd learned a thing or two during his seven years 'work experience' in the coalfields. Not least that any little inference suggesting that the miscreant had yet to accept that the individual was subordinate to the state would be noted down and remain on the miscreant's file in perpetuity. Questioning anything, even a factual error, was likely to set his rehabilitation back years.

But twenty? Could they really be that worried he could still revert to type?

Apparently so. Despite not putting one foot wrong since that one tiny *faux pas*, here he still was, still attached to the Xinhua News Agency and still never so much as smiling, even when confronted with the most ludicrous examples of China's presentation of itself in a light that never shone anything less than brilliantly.

It was a description of Xinhua Xi hadn't needed to concoct. He was all but fed it at his induction into the concrete monolith that served as the agency's Beijing HQ but looked designed to resemble the headstone of all the lost souls who'd ever entered it, never to be seen again on the stage of serious journalism.

'Xinhua means New China and that's what we're here to ensure the world understands,' said the woman in the shabby blue skirt conducting the induction, 'that it's new. That China has moved on from the China of old, even though much of the old is still relevant to the new. Indeed, that the old represents the foundation for the new which is what we at Xinhua are charged with getting across to all our new friends across the world. That they're now dealing with a China that's both old and new at the same time. Understand?'

Xi sat there, eyes glazing over as the woman continued in this vein for another hour and a half. In all that time not once did she mention Xi's precise role in all this presenting and by the time she'd repeated herself five times and it was all becoming a bit much even for her, all he knew about his new 'job' was that he was joining the ten thousand others in the Xinhua family who together had a joint responsibility for seeing that the 'new' message was disseminated loud and clear.

'Well,' thought Xi as he was led from a room that looked, as he well knew, not unlike the ones where people were convicted of crimes they hadn't committed, 'that shouldn't be too difficult. It's clear that everything about China is new... except, perhaps, the furniture, the walls, the fittings, the people and the minds that come with them. Apart from that, it looks like there've been big changes while I've been away.'

* * *

Xi's personal change came in the form of pretty much everything around him. After seven years on top of a coal mountain, out on the core sample drilling rigs or deep in the frozen depths of the core sample logging office, the Xinhua newsroom could not have been more different.

For a start he had a chair, something that was as foreign to Xi workwise as being cooped up indoors. When you'd spent your entire working life to date standing and never sat without being told to, Xi was left wondering what the protocol was in his current situation.

Just keep standing, he decided. Sit and risk the wrath of the pit boss – correction – department supervisor.

So there he'd stood, looking at the chair and the cubicle he was being expected to work from until the supervisor had come to his rescue.

'Something wrong?' the man had asked.

Xi's mouth moved but nothing came out. Apart from the chair, he now had two other issues jostling for pole position in his mind. How to react to concern for his well-being – something that'd been about as common as chairs in the coalfields – and, far more worrying, whether his re-education training to date had had a far greater effect on him than he'd realised. From nowhere, the thought had materialised that sitting down to work was in some way revisionist.

It'd taken a full week for Xi's concerns to subside sufficiently for him to be able to sink unhesitatingly on to the chair. Two for someone to tell him what he was supposed to be doing while sitting on it.

For that entire time, Xi had just sat there taking papers out of in his inbox, casting an untutored eye over them and placing them unaltered in his outbox for collection by an anonymous entity who never once offered any comment on the procedure. With no one apparently interested in giving him guidance on the job he'd been brought in to do, Xi decided his best course of action was to do no more than continue doing what he was doing and leave questions to others. After his 'I'm a geologist' gaffe, drawing attention to himself wasn't top of his list of priorities.

It had taken until the end of his second week of effectively doing nothing for it to emerge that the tactic had one fatal flaw. His supervisor's presence at his shoulder with a question to ask confirmed it. Had Xi not noticed the glaring typographical error in the story he was waving under Xi's nose?

Xi looked from the paper to the supervisor's fleshy florid face and back again, unsure how to respond. The one thing he'd learned from his term in the coalfields was that direct questions usually inferred criticism and that to respond with equal directness normally resulted in punishment for a display of surliness. In such situations, Xi had learned that the best way to avoid retribution was to say nothing, avoid looking his interrogator in the eye and adopt the most humble body posture one could muster under the circumstances.

To Xi's amazement, the tactic seemed to have the desired effect. Rather than being bawled out, his supervisor first echoed Xi's silence then, very politely, asked if it might be possible for Xi to spend a moment or two longer on each article he was checking and make a note in the margin if anything looked amiss.

At first Xi thought about answering but then thought better of it. He'd also been on the receiving end of such cynical ploys in the coalfields – a tactic resorted to by some of the trickier bosses who used unexpected civil courtesy to get him to speak up and then use his words against him.

So no, Xi thought. He wouldn't be falling for that one again and with a supreme effort did no more than continue looking silently at his shoes while bracing himself for the torrent of abuse that always followed such acts of passive non-reaction in the coalfields.

It never came. As Xi cringed under his supervisor's enquiring eye, to his astonishment all he did was look at Xi for a moment, sigh heavily and finally walk away. No bawling out. No admonishment. Not even a bout of finger jabbing.

Why? In the coalfields, repercussion was inevitable no matter what steps you took to avoid it.

It was a question that was to haunt Xi for over a year, an answer only arriving once the improvement in Xi's work had resulted in a degree of guarded familiarity developing between Xi and his supervisor.

At the end of one particularly harrowing shift, one in which Xi had noticed the man adding strong liquor to his usual green tea, that degree of familiarity on the supervisor's side had mutated into a display of almost comradely fellowship.

'Never let yourself get trapped like me, Xi,' the supervisor had slurred conspiratorially to the man he now clearly viewed as something of a confidante. 'If you do, you'll never get out. You'll be here for ever doing the same mind-numbing thing til you die and doing what I'm doing,' he said with a shake of his flask in Xi's direction. 'It's the only thing that dulls the pain.

'You probably don't realise it but in a way you were partly to blame for driving me to it, d'you know that? Remember that day I had to put you straight about your editing duties?'

As usual, Xi had just blinked non-committally at the man. They might be work colleagues but Xi had long ago learned to stay alert for tripwires woven into questions put to him by his superiors.

'Yeah, 'course you do,' said the supervisor. 'It was the day you refused to respond to my questions and all I could do was walk away. Your reaction all but told me I was wasting my time in this job and there was nothing I could do about it. When they don't give you the power to select the people you work with it was the only thing I could do. For all I knew you could've been the dim-witted son of high-up official who'd pulled strings to get him a job here. That's why I had to let it go. Shouting you out could have ended up far worse for me than it was for you.'

Poor man, thought Xi as his supervisor's head dropped at the memory. He's as much of a prisoner as I am.

The supervisor's follow-up confirmed it.

'So I couldn't get heavy and I couldn't get rid of you. Without any say in who gets the copy checker posts and no way of knowing if you were up to the job there was only one option left open to me – making sure you only got stories that no one would ever read. Well, no one except you. Remember?'

Oh yes, thought Xi. I remember that all right.

Still fearful of the backlash that was likely to come his way should he find himself over or under-stepping the mark, after his 'dressing down' by the supervisor Xi had resolved to take the man's words to heart and read every story with the sort of care a newly-qualified doctor gives his patients. Result – a pile of stories in his inbox to rival the coal mountain he'd once been forced to work on, an outbox more useful for the storing of paperclips and looks of increasing frustration from a supervisor whose patience was clearly wearing thin.

He also remembered the day the man's patience had snapped. And the surprise of being addressed in a way he'd never been addressed in the coalfields.

'Mr Xi,' the supervisor had said through obviously gritted teeth, 'while I am honoured that you have taken my guiding words to heart, it is perhaps possible that I might not have explained myself properly – something for which I take full responsibility. Thus, if you will allow me, perhaps I might be given the opportunity of redeeming myself…?'

Xi remembered being incapable of doing anything other than stare wide-eyed at him.

'While I fully appreciate the importance of ensuring that everything released from this agency to the outside world receives our full attention and arrives blemish-free under the reader's eye, it is possible that I have over-stated the position a little. While aiming at all times to adhere to the principle of accuracy, I might not have dwelt fully on the issue of timeliness.

'Whilst not like shovelling coal,' he'd said, pausing slightly on noticing Xi's mouth dropping agape, 'the work of a news agency is strongly related to the swift release of news and thus to the swiftness of pen of its valued workers. That being the case, if you'd be so kind, perhaps you'd care to revisit the degree of thought each story is given…? Oh, and if you'd also be so kind, would it be possible for you to see your way to adding your signature to all edited copy? Thank you.'

'Bloody hell,' Xi had thought, his lower jaw hanging round his feet as the supervisor smiled a smile of sweet gentility, turned and went back to his desk. 'You cynical old bastard.'

He'd heard of the good cop, bad cop tactic of making suspected felons cooperate but until now had never experienced it. Here, undoubtedly, was the good cop interlude intended to be as diametrically opposed as possible to the dressing down treatment he'd had at the hands of the coalfield bosses.

Not only had the supervisor let him know in no uncertain terms that he knew more about Xi's earlier life than he'd previously let on, but with just a few carefully chosen words he'd done what the coalfield bosses had singularly failed to do – get him on their side by treating him as someone in possession of a brain. It was almost as if the supervisor was trying to communicate a degree of respect to him.

As Xi stared into his desert campfire all these years later he found himself conjecturing that had that respect extended further than his supervisor at Xinhua, all that had transpired in subsequent years might have been very different. For a start he might not have found himself at the centre of a serious East/West contretemps, he'd likely have regained his liberty at the allotted time and would almost certainly have forever remained in blissful ignorance over just how close the world was sailing to a descent into Armageddon.

But it hadn't and neither, as it turned out, had he.

chapter nine

By the end of his tenth interminable year editing Xinhua reporter gibberish into semi-intelligible release-quality gibberish, Xi was convinced of two things. His jailers had to have forgotten about him and even life in the coalfields was better than this.

At least in the core sampling office he was using the skills he'd spent three years honing at university. Here, the grey matter hardly got exercised beyond intellectual puberty level. Faced every day with virtually identical reports of the China-glorifying posturings of the country's leaders, by the end of the first year he felt he could edit them into Xinhua-speak in his sleep.

In fact, sometimes he thought he had, his mind having left his cubicle-confined body on lengthy extraterrestrial excursions in a search for a reason why he, of all people, should have been designated to a news agency.

Sure, he'd given the coal seam exploration reports his full attention – it was about the only time he got to use his university-trained writing skills – but even so, a full transfer to Xinhua made no sense. He was a geologist, not a bloody editor, and he was supposed to be doing public service as his penance. Of what possible service his editing of Xinhua gobbledegook into grammatical Xinhua gobbledegook was to the public he had no idea. All they were were the dressed up anodyne spoutings of the clone-like pillars of the establishment which went to great lengths, in all senses of the word, not to tell the world anything of what was really going on in China.

Maybe, Xi thought, that was the point. Maybe it was another of the establishment's little jokes. 'I know,' he could imagine them saying, 'let's punish him by putting him somewhere where he can't use his skills. That'll teach the little blighter.'

Whatever their motivation, he was going to be the last to know. Of that he was certain. Less sure was how long it was going to go on. Ten years was the regular length of contract those recruited to the agency signed. Would the same be applied to him?

If anyone knew, they weren't saying and, as the end of his tenth year loomed, Xi had begun to imagine this incarceration just going on and on until he dropped off his perch.

He'd virtually resigned himself to the fact when, out of the blue, things suddenly changed. Without any warning he'd received a summons. His presence was required in the editor's office.

All the way to the twenty-first floor, Xi's imagination raced. Was this it? Was he to be told he'd done his time? That they were satisfied he'd been rehabilitated and was no longer a threat to society? Or was it the opposite? That he still had to prove himself.

Surely the former. Apart from that one little blemish on his record on being told he was being transferred from the coalfields to Xinhua, he had nothing to reproach himself for. He'd made very sure of that. Every day for that ten years he'd arrived at work from his Xinhua compound dormitory at the appointed time, had done precisely what he'd been told to do, had obediently eaten in the Xinhua canteen with all the agency's other workers when they said he could, and had hardly left the Xinhua compound in all that time. By anyone's standards he was a model worker. So how could they possibly conclude otherwise?

* * *

'I see you've done nearly ten years with us,' said the man Xi had only set eyes on a handful of times, always in the company of grey-suited officials being given the guided tour of the Xinhua newsroom.

'Yes sir,' was all Xi allowed himself to say. Anything more might be seized on as a sign of a recalcitrant self and that was the last impression Xi wanted to give... for now.

'Very well. Well, as I'm sure you're aware, after ten years every Xinhua worker is given a choice. He can choose to stay with us or go elsewhere and we'd be interested in knowing what your choice will be come the time. We're not seeking an immediate answer but would like it known that should you opt to continue with us, you would be being transferred to a different office, one some distance from here. We can give you a week to think about it.'

Xi left the office his mind in turmoil. He'd arrived expecting to at last hear whether he'd satisfied enough requirements to qualify for release to the outside world. All he'd got was a choice. One that not only failed to answer that one burning question but raised several others. From what he'd just heard he still had no idea if he could choose to walk out of the door a free man or whether he'd been told that opting not to stay would mean a transfer to some other state-run operation to complete his sentence.

As he walked preoccupied down the eighteen flights of stairs back to the newsroom his head filled with the alternatives. It was like playing Russian roulette. If he opted to go, it could be like pulling the trigger on a loaded chamber. If experience with his handlers' previous transfer decisions were anything to go by he could well find himself cleaning toilets for the rest of his life. But there was always the chance that, between the lines, the editor had been telling him his time was up.

He could, of course, go back and ask directly. But that way lay demons. Knowing that any form of direct anything was not only anathema to the Xinhua way but likely to wake the kraken, in his position that course of action was strictly the line of last resort. The choice he'd been given, Xi's inner paranoia warned him, could well be a test. One to determine whether he really had conformed to societal standards. The posing of any sort of question at this stage could well be taken that he hadn't.

Normally a sound sleeper despite the existence he'd been condemned to, Xi experienced insomnia for the first time in years. Not since that night in the cells awaiting his trial had he gone a whole night without nodding off. On the one hand…. but then on the other…

By the time he 'awoke' from his third sleepless night in a row Xi knew this was getting him nowhere and that a different course of action was required. One he knew he should have adopted from the start.

'Let the wind find you,' was all a Taoist monk had had to say on being badgered by a schoolboy Xi in torment over whether to choose love over a promising career.

'Thanks a bunch,' was Xi's unspoken response. 'I was hoping for something a little less cryptic.'

Despite no further explanation and not really getting what it was the man was trying to convey to him, the monk's words had stayed with him, playing on Xi's mind until suddenly he not only got it but knew what to do with it.

With difficulty, Xi had cleared his mind and once he had, the answer was blindingly obvious. The girl he'd been bewitched by in spite of her continuous grizzlings about being made to feel second best to his studies was clearly not for him. 'If she was,' whispered the wind in his ear, 'would she not be encouraging you, not standing in your way?'

At that time, with everything that was on it, the mind clearing exercise the monk had prescribed had taken some readjustment.

Rocks, books and the girl were what he was used to staring at. Not into space allowing the mind to settle and the wind to find him.

At his Xinhua desk it was different. Here he did it every day and still got through his work load. Mostly at one and the same time.

Even so, it took until almost the end of the week he'd been given for something like an answer to arrive. When it did, it wasn't what Xi was expecting.

'I'd suggest you stay,' said the wind.

'Really? Just like that?'

'Sure. Think about it. Extending your stay achieves three things in one. It prevents any suspicions of non-rehabilitation, saves you from any nasty shocks if you opt not to and gives you a unique opportunity to achieve what you've wanted to achieve ever since the day you were detained.'

'How so?'

'Well, so far you've done nothing to rock the boat, all in an attempt to win your release by convincing them you're no longer a threat to the established order. Well, that worked out well, didn't it? Looks to me that you're fucked no matter what you do or don't do, so why not make it work for you?

'You're on the inside, Xi. Has that not occurred to you? You're in a place that's the very epicentre of China's brainwashing machinery. If you can't find some way of making that work to your advantage vendetta-wise then I'd suggest it's time to start worrying… beginning with whether you yourself might not have fallen victim to the machine. You have been part of it for rather a long time…'

* * *

'Well?' The editor's eyes told Xi he wasn't in the mood for long, drawn out meetings with underlings. 'Have you reached a decision?'

'Yes, comrade editor,' said Xi trying not to smile. 'I'd like to stay on.'

'Excellent. Your decision to continue serving the Motherland will not go unrecognised.'

Considering that an end to the conversation, the editor's eyes returned to the papers on his desk until out of the corner of them he noticed Xi still standing there.

'Was there something else?'

'Er… if I could just ask… if you would be so kind… you did mention a different location comrade editor?'

For the first time in ten years, Xi had plucked up the courage to chance his arm. It wasn't that he was any less worried that asking questions might jeopardise his position. It was that, by showing enthusiasm to remain in service to the nation, he considered himself at least partially protected from any repercussions. And anyway, how could asking where he was to be sent be regarded as demonstrating excessive self-interest? He'd need a bit of time to prepare if Xinhua decided to dispatch him to the Chinese backwoods. Warm clothes for Mongolia or Sichuan, the opposite for Hainan or Guangzhou, a phrase book for the far west.

As concerned as he was about undoing all the good, obedient progress he'd made in trying to cement a reputation for compliance, Xi's insomnia had had the last word. It wasn't just the worry of not knowing what to expect if he turned down the staying on 'request'. It was where the 'different location' was. If he was ever to sleep again he knew he had to know. And perhaps more importantly, why?

The permutations were endless. The agency had outposts all over the country, all feeding regular reports on Party official speeches back to Beijing which, in Xi's view, was a bit like eating your own vomit.

It was from Beijing that those self-same speeches originated, speeches which would never have got anywhere near the provinces had they not first been approved by Beijing. The only reason Xinhua had staff members posted around the country, as Xi knew full well, was to check the delivery against the approved text. Deviations could signify deviation from the Party line which in itself could signify an attempt by a Party official to build his own local power base. Which was where the locally-based Xinhua 'reporters' came in.

Their presence was intended as a deterrent against such subversive acts. To make Party officials think twice before acting on the old China adage about the mountain being high and the emperor being far away.

It didn't always work. Xi knew that too. Sometimes either the Xinhua overseers were asleep on the job or had gone native, falling into league with those they were supposed to be checking on. Which was why Xinhua's head honchos carried out regular purges of their provincial representatives.

From what the editor had said, Xi could only assume that just such a purge was imminent and that a game of Xinhua personnel musical chairs was about to begin. All of which put scarcely credible thoughts in Xi's mind. Was he now considered one of the trusted few? Were they about to send him out into the field as one of the overseers?

Xi didn't know whether to be flattered or insulted. Did they really consider him so rehabilitated he was worthy of high office? If so, he'd obviously done a good job convincing them. Too good, perhaps. Maybe this too was a test of his rehabilitation. Maybe he too would be under surveillance while he was surveilling others suspected of going off-piste.

Aaaaargh. The permutations made Xi's head hurt.

Fortunately the wind came to his rescue. 'You'll never know if you don't ask, you twat,' it'd screamed through the cracks in his confused cranium leaving Xi no option but to stand his ground to effectively challenge the editor's 'meeting over' gesture.

* * *

'Location?' mumbled the editor while making a note in the margin of a file he was working on. Please God, not mine, thought Xi.

'Yes... sorry comrade editor.'

'One moment,' said the editor reaching into a desk drawer to retrieve another file. 'Hmmm. Yes. A different location,' he said after browsing the file's contents. 'This is correct.'

Xi watched him replace the file and make to return to the papers on his desk.

Oh shit. Ah well, in for a penny, thought Xi.

'Sorry comrade editor but might I trouble you for an indication of the location of that location...?' Jeez, he thought, that was brazen. Ah well, out now.

'Location?' said the editor.

'Yes, you pea-brained twat-head. We've been through that. Don't make me wring it out of you,' Xi just stopped himself shouting at the puffed-up prick behind the desk who was clearly under the impression that authority could only be properly demonstrated if it involved making the lives of others a misery. Instead, he restricted himself to an almost imperceptible nod of the head.

After a pause to cast a stone-eyed look to ensure the underling standing in front of him got the message that he was about to be done a great favour, the editor sighed deeply and retrieved the file once more.

'Yes. You are to be sent to another Xinhua office. One some distance from Beijing,' and moved to put the file back in the drawer.

70

Enough, thought Xi.

'WHERE...er... please, comrade editor?' he said out loud.

Comrade editor stopped, looked hard at Xi then down at the file, turned some pages, turned them back, ran his finger down various lists, scratched his head, took a sip of tea, turned more pages, consulted another file, then looked back at the first file and finally up at Xi, a malicious smirk playing on his lips.

'Africa,' he said.

chapter ten

As the thought struck, Gideon Kariuki afforded himself a small chuckle. Although his flock wouldn't know it, the word 'godsend' in his oratory would be carrying more meanings than one. Yes, he was quite sincere about them being sent by God. But what they'd never know was just how much of a godsend they were to him personally. Without the scraps of intelligence they delivered daily, not only would he be facing ecclesiastical and professional disgrace but financial ruin into the bargain.

Put together, those scraps had provided the foundation for a plan that was very shortly to see heaven replace impending hell in the Kariuki firmament. Thanks to their tip-offs, and what Moses had brought him, no longer would he or his church have cause to quake every time a police siren screamed. He had his 'get out of hell' card securely stashed and all that remained was to cash it in with the relevant parties.

Yes, those parties might be a godless swarm of heathen locusts intent on gorging their way across Africa, but Kariuki had consulted his Lord on the deal and had so far heard nothing to make him think again. So far as the Almighty was concerned, it seemed He deemed it excusable behaviour. In fact, thought Kariuki, the silence could be construed not only as showing no objection to the practice but of actually condoning it. Kariuki could even imagine the Lord smiling on being made aware of Kariuki's stratagem for channelling funds out of the pockets of the devil incarnate and into the coffers of those willing to sacrifice themselves for the fulfilment of His grand plan.

'Thank you Lord,' muttered Kariuki to the heavens. 'With Your blessing, how can I fail? With You to guide me Lord, the God-fearing African people will soon be consigning the Chinese antichrist to the fires of everlasting damnation and preserving not only the sanctity of the church but the very fabric of Africa itself.'

Hmmm, he thought. Not bad. Might work that into my sermon. Maybe best not to mention the Chinese by name though. Don't want to draw attention to the victim whose pockets are going to get picked to keep the church afloat. Some of my flock might not see it the way the Lord and I do.

It was the word 'fabric' that prompted Pastor Kariuki's hesitation. With any number of his church's devotees engaged in a textile industry currently being decimated by cheap Chinese imports, Our Saviour's Church of Number One Good Samaritans could well witness an outright rebellion were it to become public knowledge that the church's future hinged on diverting Chinese state funds into the church's account.

It was a point of view Kariuki understood completely. His flock weren't the only ones with firsthand experience of seeing the Chinese suck the soul out of the African entrepreneur. Hardly any of Kariuki's own investments had escaped a mauling at the hands of the continent's latest invader.

One in particular made Kariuki's lip curl.

'Bastards,' he muttered under his breath hoping the Lord would understand. 'The unspeakable shits. No one does that to me. No one.'

It wasn't just what they'd done but the way they'd done it that had Kariuki clenching and unclenching his fists. For bare-faced brazen duplicity it left all other betrayals standing and Kariuki in a state of confused paroxysm. He didn't know which was worse.

Being the victim of a truly villainous act of treachery or trying not to admire the Chinese for their utter, complete and unfettered ruthlessness in the way they conducted business.

Here in Africa it was a given that you trusted no one other than close family members and even then you had to sleep with your hand on your wallet. But at least with the African you could generally tell when he was about to sting you. Dollars signs lit up in his eyes.

Not so with the Chinese. Even when delivering their *coup de grâce*, their eyes betrayed nothing. No passion, no emotion, no triumph. All you got, as Kariuki knew to his cost, was the unblinking, stone-eyed look of the executioner. The one that said he had no feelings one way or the other on the matter. He had a job to do and was simply there to do it. End of.

Even so, Kariuki reprimanded himself for not seeing it coming. He knew the Chinese were talking to the Mombasa mayor's 'special' advisor, a man of infamy known to all as the Sheikh who effectively ruled the roost in the ancient coastal city. Why hadn't he twigged that they were colluding to deprive Kariuki's company of the fruits of a highly profitable enterprise? Had all those years laying its foundations made him and the company's senior management complacent? Very possibly.

Actually, almost definitely. When the axe finally fell, neither Kariuki nor the company's Australian CEO could quite believe it. They thought they had a deal with the Chinese. Kariuki's mining company dug the titanium ore out of the Shimba Hills and the men from Guangdong bought it once it reached China. Granted they'd also underwritten the loans the company had secured with Kariuki's bank to keep the diggers digging, but other than that they had no input other than to monitor progress with the project.

Or so Kariuki had thought.

The scales fell from his eyes the day the dedicated handling terminals built to bypass the Mombasa port chaos and cut weeks off the company's shipments to China were finished. Within minutes of the inaugural shipment being loaded and the ship made ready to sail, the company received a note from the Sheikh's office. There were irregularities in the titanium export papers, irregularities that needed to be ironed out before the ship could be allowed out of port.

Kariuki was only too aware of what that meant. It meant that the mayor's henchman was pushing his luck. Knowing he had the company over a barrel, he was demanding an additional 'something small' over and above the series of small somethings the company had already paid to get this far along the wholly fabricated obstacle course of bureaucratic red tape.

Made aware of the new demands, Kariuki had sighed resignedly, grabbed an overnight bag and a bulging briefcase he kept on hand for eventualities like this, and headed for the airport.

* * *

'Do come in,' smiled the snake inhabiting the special advisor's voluminous chair on the far side of a football field-sized desk. 'Something to drink after your long journey? *Chai? Kahawa? Fanta?* You'll understand I have nothing more fortifying to offer you.'

Kariuki lowered his bulky frame gingerly on to the fragile stickwood chair his host deliberately placed on the visitors' side of the desk to remind them who was who in his office and pointedly placed the briefcase on the expanse that separated the two men.

'Let's just get this over with shall we?' said Kariuki wearily. 'I've come a long way at short notice to mediate in this delicate matter and I'd very much like to get the relevant paperwork to the ship's captain today.'

'Of course, of course, *rafiki*. Your haste is quite understandable. Your consignee will be wondering why the ship missed the tide. But I would ask for your understanding in return. As I'm sure you're well aware, there are procedures to adhere to in matters of this nature and unless they're followed to the letter both I and the mayor's office could be deemed culpable. As a minister of your church and a respected pillar of the community I'm sure you wouldn't want to find yourself responsible for the consequences we could face were it to be discovered that something crucial had been overlooked.'

Kariuki got the message. His adversary knew the strength of his position and wasn't about to squander a gold-plated opportunity to squeeze Kariuki until his eyes popped. Eventually an 'understanding' would be reached but not until the snake had had its fun. Kariuki knew he could expect nothing less than the gradual tightening of the serpent's coils until he was begging for mercy, not just financially but politically. Apart from having no option but to contribute generously to the Sheikh's 'benevolent fund' Kariuki knew he was about to be subjected to a reminder of the power vested in the mayoral office's highest-ranking incumbents by the local electorate.

'Bloody politics,' grumbled Kariuki to himself. 'Why does it always have to intervene in business in this damned country?'

But intervene it did, frequently and unerringly, and when it involved two power mongers from opposite sides of the political divide jousting for control of a given situation, as on this occasion, there was only ever going to be one loser... modernisation of a backward economy.

'It's not even as if we're that different,' Kariuki had thought ruefully. 'We're both capitalist-minded. We both believe in the benefits of freeing-up business to help develop the economy and raise the underprivileged out of poverty. Neither of us has Marxist-

Leninist leanings. So why can't we just agree to disagree on the minor points and collaborate to get the job done?'

Kariuki didn't need an answer. He knew as well as anyone there was something way more fundamental than simple politics blocking collaboration for the common good. When the various parties were aligned along tribal, rather than political, lines – dubbed the triblical dimension by the local media – and historic hatred between the major tribes superseded all other considerations in the Kenyan parliament, the national interest was always going to come off second best.

Although the point of contention between Kariuki and his current adversary wasn't outwardly triblical, Kariuki was under no illusion that that's exactly what his Swahili host intended making it. Being seen to have put a reviled Kikuyu in his place would do his political ambitions no harm at all come the next election. He might even attract support from other Kikuyu-loathing tribes inhabiting a coastal province convinced it was being deprived of regional development funding by Kenya's Kikuyu-dominated government.

Facing that sort of opposition, Kariuki knew he was on a hiding to nothing the moment the man began taking an interest in his titanium shipping project. In the Sheikh's eyes Kariuki represented everything the minor tribes despised and resented. Not only had Kikuyus like Kariuki grown fat on the fruits of the fertile Kenyan highlands while the sixty-something other tribes had had to make do with the leftovers but, by sheer dint of numbers, Kenya's biggest tribe had manipulated affairs to rule the political roost almost uninterrupted since independence in 1963.

On the face of it, the Kikuyu looked invulnerable. But that, oddly, is where his current opponent and Kariuki shared a common belief. Both knew the dynasty could be brought to an abrupt end should the other tribes ever manage to forge a lasting alliance and both knew what the repercussions would be if they did. Which was why the Kikuyu elders pored long and hard over strategies designed to make sure that eventuality never came to pass.

If there was one thing the Kikuyu knew about it was the principle of divide and rule. After decades of practice they had it down to a fine art. If they couldn't win friends by appealing to the smaller tribes' sense of avarice, they had the resources to inject enmity instead, especially between the minor tribes and the Luo, the one tribe capable of challenging the Kikuyu's dominance given the support of other tribes.

With centuries of bad blood between them, spilling over into brutal bouts of bloodletting at times, the prospect of a Luo victory at the polls was responsible for keeping Kariuki awake at night. The recurrent nightmare featuring the recrimination the Kikuyu would have heaped on them in the aftermath of such an event left Kariuki waking in a cold sweat even though, as he knew, it was about as likely as Kenya being subjected to a nationwide ban on alcohol.

Until recently it was a parallel Kariuki found comforting. Nothing was less likely. There'd be riots in the streets. But in recent years, that comfort factor had waned in direct proportion to the rise of a new force in the land, one whose simple presence could indeed make the unthinkable become a highly unpalatable reality.

While most in the ruling clique shrugged it off as a here today gone tomorrow fad, to Kariuki there were two specific reasons why writing the new force off was a big mistake. Apart from representing a major threat to Kenya's Christian ethic, the growing Islamic fundamentalist movement cut across tribal boundaries, unifying disparate tribes under one banner. Leaving the movement alone to cement itself on the Kenyan landscape would put not only the religion he followed at risk but the strategy the Kikuyu employed for maintaining their stranglehold on power.

To date, having never been in the presence of anyone admitting to be a fundamentalist, Kariuki's concern had only been theoretical.

All that changed the moment he set foot in the Sheikh's office. No one symbolised the movement's ethos better than the man sitting the other side of a desk that personified the extent of the gulf between them.

chapter eleven

By the end of his meeting with the Sheikh, Kariuki was relieved
no alcohol ban had yet been imposed on Mombasa. After
what he'd just been told he needed several very large whisky and
sodas. But as he downed the first of them, slumped in a sagging
armchair on the terrace of the venerable old colonial Mombasa
Club, he wondered how much longer he and his fellow members
had before such behaviour was deemed *haram*.

Looking around him, all he saw was genteel bonhomie and good
natured banter as the club's members genially toasted one another's
health and good fortune. Gazing over their heads towards the old
Portuguese Fort stoically guarding the harbour and the glittering
Indian Ocean beyond, he wished he could participate in the jollity.
But unlike them, Kariuki had just been shown a future which would
have had them gagging on their G&Ts had they too been privy to
it. It was a future in which such jovial comradeship wasn't just
outlawed, it was judged profane heresy.

Although his adversary hadn't spelled it out, Kariuki could tell
from his eyes, beard and robes what was in his mind. In the
Mombasa of the future there would be no place for heretical relics
like the fort, the club or its members. In their place would stand
monster shopping malls, alcohol-free amusement parks and
golden-domed mosques catering for the every need of an increas-
ingly Islamicised populace and none of the infidel invader's. It was
time, the eyes had told him, to reclaim the city from the grasp of
those who'd turned it into a modern day Sodom and Gomorrah.

What's more, with the help of the Sheikh's new friends from the East, it was beginning to look like the avenging angel would be arriving on the club's doorstep a lot sooner than any of its members could ever dare imagine. Kariuki, the creationist believer in the literal meaning of the Bible, blanched inwardly at the thought.

'Looks like you could do with another of those mate,' twanged the outback tones of the Australian who'd just joined him. 'Good meeting was it?'

Kariuki looked up into the weather-beaten face of the mining company's CEO and sighed heavily.

'Educational,' he said. 'I feel like I've been in a tutorial with the devil incarnate.'

'Know what you mean. The man's a firebrand and no mistake. But in the end he's still just a man. And we both know that in this neck of the woods there's not an ocker amongst 'em who doesn't have his price. How much was his?'

'More than I had on me.'

The Australian froze with his beer halfway to his lips. That's not what he was expecting to hear. On receiving Kariuki's call he'd raced over from the loading terminal hoping to be on his way back in seconds, all paperwork signed and sealed and ready for inspection by the harbourmaster. If the ship missed the next tide as well, there'd be some serious kowtowing to do at the feet of the Chinese buyer of the company's first shipment.

'So where does that leave us?' managed the Australian after a moment to recover from what he hoped was a Kariuki tease.

'In a very bad place,' returned Kariuki in a tone that left the CEO in no doubt that it wasn't. 'It would seem that we missed something, my friend. Did you pick up on how the Chinese were chummying up to him?'

'Well, yeah, but I thought that was the Chinks way of smarming themselves into the mayor's good books to get in on all the construction work he's got planned. There'll be some mighty rich pickings to be had once that gets underway… not to mention the soft power peddling potential of getting him to agree to let them fund it with Chinese cash.'

'Well it would seem that China's charm offensive is working out better for them than we thought. Not only is Mombasa on the brink of seeing an army of Chinese workers tearing it apart and reconstructing it in the image of the Prophet but certain port activities are about to be put under Chinese control, ours included unless we can come up with a ransom that'd make King Solomon wince.'

With the Australian struck dumb for once it was left to Kariuki to expand on the details. Stripped down to its essentials, it was now clear that the Chinese company they'd signed a titanium ore supply deal with wasn't just an ore importer. It was the front for a far bigger group that wasn't satisfied with regular supplies of titanium alone. To make such supplies secure it was after complete control of the entire mining and shipping operation.

'Effectively, after having done all the hard yards, our operation is facing a takeover by a Chinese group that's using all its pulling power with the relevant authorities to ensure they get it for a song. I've just been informed that the harbour fees have been increased…. to a level that makes the shipments hopelessly uneconomic.

'This,' said Kariuki handing the Australian a sheet of paper, 'is what they're now demanding. Not just for the first shipment. For every shipment.'

'Holy fuck… 'scuse the language Pastor… but there's no way we can factor that in. No buyer in the world is going to pay the sort of premium we'd have to incorporate to cover that sort of outlay. Is there nothing we can do?'

'Two things as I see it. We can fight it in the courts but you and I both know how long that'd take… and anyway the judiciary is as corrupt as the Sheikh. Or we could make the man an offer he can't refuse. But then we'd more than likely have the likes of the Triads and the Sheikh's fundamentalist friends to deal with.'

'So... what you're saying then... is... that we're fucked? Sorry.'

'Right up the proverbial by the looks of it,' said Kariuki draining his drink, leaning back resignedly in his chair and waving his glass in the air to catch the steward's attention. If the Sheikh really had the Chinese one hundred percent onside, that'd mean he'd soon have access to the sort of firepower needed to put both his political campaign and his subsequent Mombasa remodelling plan into action. And just in case that plan was already being unfurled, Kariuki was determined to make as much use of the bar as possible before the club, Mombasa and the whole of the coast province fell victim to the Sheikh's ultimate intention – the introduction of Sharia law.

* * *

In the end, the Sheikh's collusion with the Chinese had had twin effects. Not only had Kariuki and his Australian partners been forced to hand over a controlling interest in the mining operation to the Chinese for a peppercorn price but by doing so both the Sheikh and the entire Chinese nation had made a powerful new enemy.

It was the bare-faced underhand skulduggery about how they went about it that had Kariuki seeing the deepest red.

Even in Africa people largely respected contracts. To the Chinese such legal documents seemed to represent nothing more than a deal-breaker's checklist.

One by one they reneged on mutually binding agreements culminating in the *coup de grâce*, the withdrawal of their under-writing guarantee of the mining company's loan from Kariuki's bank. Without that, the bank was forced to call in a loan the joint Kariuki/Australian mining operation couldn't cover without selling out to a Chinese buyer with a name not dissimilar to the purchaser of the titanium shipments.

And then the dirty icing on the dirtiest of dirty cakes. Within hours of the buy-out completion, the harbour fees were cut to manageable proportions.

In truth, by the time the revised fees were announced, Kariuki expected nothing less. The big surprise would've been if the Sheikh had left them as they were.

'Well,' thought Kariuki as he recalled the whole tooth-grinding saga from the vantage point of his sermon-writing desk in his church office, 'if it's surprises the Chinese are into, they'll love the one I've got in store for them.'

Glancing over at the safe which held the little package Moses had presented to him, Kariuki smiled inwardly. There are two sides to every scam, he thought, and the Chinese were about to discover just how resourceful the African could be when it came to the balancing of books on that score, a resourcefulness for which, on this occasion, Kariuki had an unlikely source to thank.

Had it not been for the bush-ravaged Irishman in dire need of a haircut, a new razorblade, a jacket that fitted and funds for a hare-brained solar energy scheme who'd accosted him at a World Bank meeting in Nairobi some years before, Kariuki would not now be in a position to more than atone for his humiliation at the hands of Africa's latest colonial wannabe.

* * *

Kariuki dreaded such meetings. They brought him into contact with people like Kearney who had nothing on their minds other than trying to get their hands on the contents of his wallet.

But to people like Kariuki they were an unfortunate occupational hazard. As a senior representative of one of the banks chosen by the Kenyan government and foreign aid donors to channel funds to development projects, he could hardly get out of them. Not only that, but on occasion he found himself obligated to present papers at such meetings, something that instantly made him a target for leeches like the grubby Irishman.

Fortunately for Kariuki, having had to attend so many such events he was well versed in the procedure for dealing with uninvited intrusions into his private, well-guarded world of high finance. After giving Kearney the regulation forty-five seconds of his time, he'd expressed a wholly-disingenuous interest, told the man to send a detailed summary of the project to his office through the proper channels and turned back to discussing with those of his own ilk whether they could expect black or red caviar for lunch.

Kariuki knew from the man's dropped jaw on being asked to produce something in writing that he'd never hear from him again.

He was right. Nothing ever did appear and the name Kearney had been consigned to Kariuki's mental waste bin.

Or so Kariuki had thought. Years later it was clear a residue remained. A residue Kariuki could only think must have been the result of what the man had said on accosting him. Apart from the details of the scheme itself – which, Kariuki had grudgingly admitted to himself, did, in the right hands, have an outside chance of being something of a money-spinner – it was the way Kearney had introduced himself.

'Anthony Kearney,' said the Irishman holding out his hand to Kariuki. 'People call me Kal.'

The blank, silent, handshake-less look Kearney got in response had failed to have the effect Kariuki intended. Rather than receiving it as an invitation to bugger off and go find someone else to bother, Kearney had taken it as one to expand on the name.

'It's from my email address,' he'd said before Kariuki could stop him. 'When I was looking for memorable name I discovered no one was using my initials with 47 after them so I grabbed it quick. So, AK47... Kalashnikov... Kal. It's an Irish thing.'

If nothing else, the story had had the effect of indelibly printing the name Kearney on the minds of his audience, on this occasion that of the somewhat under-impressed, Savile Row-suited finance director of the bank Kearney was trying to tap for funds to get his project off the ground.

Having listened briefly to Kearney's presentation and given him the regulation brush-off, that's the last Kariuki expected to hear of him. But when the name had reappeared unexpectedly on Kariuki's radar some years later, a file the banker had thought long-deleted opened in his subconscious.

'Kearney... Kearney... ' muttered Kariuki when Moses had mentioned the name. 'Yes. Think I came across him once. Some sort of safari lowlife isn't he?'

'Yes *mzee*. He runs Kearney's Kenya. It's a company a lot of people know because of its logo... KK.'

Kariuki had to smile. Kearney obviously had a talent for choosing names that stuck. KK was the abbreviation of *kitu kidogo*, the 'something small' Kiswahili euphemism for an illegal inducement heard at least once a day every day by every person in Kenya.

Yes, Kearney had a talent for names all right. But maybe this was a name too far. The Irishman obviously hadn't factored in that the logo could have a serious business-restricting downside. No one who knew what KK signified was ever going to be seen travelling in a vehicle as much as advertising the company's degree of respect for the law. It would draw unwanted attention to them.

So why, thought Kariuki, were the Chinese using it? If, as Moses had told him, the Chinese embassy had specifically sought KK out to run their safaris, what could possibly be their motivation? There were plenty of way more respectable companies around not only not saddled with the KK connotation but who'd give their eye teeth to get a slice of the Chinese pie. It didn't make sense. Either the Chinese didn't know what KK meant or they were up to something and with the grudge he still held for the Chinese still festering in his chest Kariuki knew he'd never rest easy until he knew what. Somewhere in this could be a way to deliver divine retribution on those who would seek to unseat him.

How, though, to learn more? Moses might be able to glean a few indicators via his part-time employment as a driver for the Nairobi bureau of China's state news agency but Kariuki knew he'd never get close enough to the chiefs to get a definitive answer.

So no, this was no job for an amateur. This needed a specialist. Someone who could infiltrate and cajole an answer out of those in the know.

There was only one person sufficiently qualified. Kariuki's sister-in-law could not only match Kariuki for avarice but knew how to apply her charms to satisfy her voracious physical needs.

There was only one problem. She had a quite understandable aversion to the Chinese. To Beatrice Kinyui, even the Luo were less detestable than the Chinaman. At least they had the wherewithal to conduct themselves in a manly fashion.

So if Kariuki was hoping she'd agree to work the honey trap with the men from the embassy he knew he'd be asking the wrong person.

The *mzungu*, on the other hand, were a different matter. Not unfamiliar with Kinyui's weakness for the white man, Kariuki knew he'd be on firmer ground asking her to 'befriend' a hunky, red-blooded Irishman with a libido the size of Mount Kenya.

'Who knows,' Kariuki mused, 'I might even get a discount.'

chapter twelve

It might have been the heat. It might have been the dizzying, intoxicating scent of the frangipani blossoms hanging suffocatingly in the fetid night air. But most likely, thought Kearney on reflection, it was the drink that had them tearing at one another's clothes like hormonal teenagers in the back of the Falcon before spotting a pair of eyes looking at them from the bushes and freezing in mid-tear.

Swallowed up by the moment, neither Kearney nor Beatrice Kinyui had noticed the *askari* night watchman creeping into the car park's lush undergrowth to do what he thought his job description required him to do – watch.

If he'd left it at that, his presence would likely have gone undetected. But when the bushes started twitching erratically in the heavy motionless air there was only one conclusion the Falcon's occupants could draw. Someone was exceeding his job description requirements by some margin.

Clambering hastily back into their clothes, Kearney and Kinyui caught the look in one another's eye and simultaneously collapsed into splutterings of helpless mirth. The look on the poor man's face as Kearney's flashlight startled the voyeur into crashing headlong out of the bushes, ambushed by the very trousers he was trying to pull up – priceless.

By the time they'd readjusted themselves and got their splutterings under control, the man was long gone leaving them staring at one another and wondering how, exactly, that had happened.

One moment they were walking calmly across the car park to their respective vehicles, Ryan off on what Kearney thought he heard the man describe as an African tiger hunt, the next they were clawing at one another's buttons and zips in the back of Kearney's Landrover.

There'd been no preliminary skirmishing. Just full-on all-out consumption before the eyes of either could blink. Eyes, they now realised, which had exchanged a lot more than just exasperation as the idiot American professor was occupied in digging his own grave.

Now those same sets of eyes were exchanging yet more information.

'You know I'm married,' said the one.

'Don't care,' said the other.

'Oh God,' said the first.

'You're sexual dynamite,' came the reply.

'Oh GOD!' said the recipient's.

'Not quite, but close,' glinted Kearney's in the dim car park lights.

'Gotta go,' said Kinyui's, tearing herself away from the exchange and fumbling for the door.

Wrenching it open, Kinyui leaped raggedly out into the night and all but ran towards her own car, Kearney watching through bleary, sex-sodden slits feeling only shellshock. She'd bombed him in a night raid and without a word was about to return to base leaving nothing but a man spent.

Nothing, that is, except for the business card on the seat she'd just vacated.

Accident? Design? Accident? The question haunted him all the way home. Had it fallen unnoticed from her bag during her post-coital car key hunt or was there more to it than that?

Kearney's mind churned as he tried to visualise the moment before she'd fled knowing all the while that now wasn't the time for such thoughts. Having the word 'accident' pounding in your brain as you headed out into the African bush three-fifths drunk at dead of night on a road notorious for carjackings wasn't the best way of tackling such an expedition – especially when the Falcon's headlights, for no explicable reason, had just started flickering.

*   *   *

Half way home on a desolate stretch still miles from the shack he rented in the Ngong Hills fringing Nairobi's southern outskirts, the event the flickering portended came alarmingly to fruition leaving Kearney no option but to grab the flashlight and start poking around under the hood.

As he did so, two thoughts flashed through his mind.

One, that it was just a matter of time before the night raiders sniffed him out to make off with his pride and joy leaving him battered and bruised… or worse.

Two, that those on his Catholic father's side would argue that he only had himself to blame. Taking advantage of a married woman with one too many glasses of wine inside her, indeed! God's vengeance would know no bounds.

Oddly, as he fiddled with various connections in the engine compartment trying to keep the rising panic under control and ignore the nagging voice of God replacing the word 'accident' in his head, a strange feeling of calm spread through him, the sort he'd heard washed over you while drowning. There was, he knew, nothing that could be done about the situation other than deal with it and, just as you did while drowning, revel in the images of your past life flashing before your eyes.

In Kearney's case there were a lot more to revel in than the average drowning man's. Born into a family ostracised from Irish community courtesy of his father's entanglement with a woman from the wrong side of the religious tracks, he'd grown up in a small town close to the border with the North having to look over his shoulder wherever he went. Friends he could trust could be counted on the kneecaps of an IRA squealer leaving Kearney no option but to find friendship in things that were less judgemental.

In Kearney's world, stones and bones became the closest thing to a band of brothers he could feel at home with. To Kearney, not only were rocks, plants and animals about the only things in Ireland not tainted with the religion absurdity but they never interrupted when he was talking and never offered advice that hadn't been asked for.

When it was, Kearney listened and it was just such a piece of advice that saw the young Irishman boarding a plane to Australia on a mission to complete his education.

'Go,' his confidantes urged. 'Get as far away from this place as possible. There's nothing for you here except prejudice, suspicion and rank disdain. Go somewhere where cultural mash-up is the norm, not the persecuted exception. Be gone and don't come back until the only church left in this place is the Church of the Darwinian Disciple. Stay and be sure of being marked down as the heretic the priests will undoubtedly point to when scaring little children into reading the litany. Stay and be sure of becoming the antichrist destined to spend eternity fuelling the fires of hell. Or worse, an American creationist's central heating boiler.'

Three years of following the advice to the letter later and Kearney had his passport to the rest of the world, a geology degree that was to win him his first real job with a company that had no serious intention of helping its Ethiopian hosts find oil.

Two years it had taken Kearney and Ryan to realise it and once they had, nothing was going to stop the pair jumping ship to seek their fortunes elsewhere.

Five years of disappointment in that department and Kearney

had reached the stage at which he needed a distraction, one he'd found in the beguiling shape of a Somali girl living in Nairobi.

Besotted with the girl to the point of intoxication he'd ended up marrying her in a tribal ceremony with Islamic undertones and less than twelve months later had come home to a house stripped of everything bar a healthy population of mosquitoes and a feral cat ferociously guarding its kittens.

It wasn't as if he hadn't been warned.

Grinning from ear to ear as Kearney recounted the tale of coming in from the bush after a week away to find no *askari* on the gate, the house in total darkness, all doors missing and not even a bottle opener left to open the beer that wasn't in the fridge that wasn't there, Ryan's reaction was to order a round of the most expensive drinks and pass the bill to his countryman.

'Dis yous owes me,' he'd said, lifting his glass to toast his own perspicacity. At Kearney's own stag night he'd bet the groom it wouldn't last a year.

'Yous knows as well as oi do dat Somali terts are as shifty as dey're feckin' beautiful,' he'd told Kearney to his face with a candour Kearney would have found disturbing had he been listening properly.

'Yous isn't just marryin' der girl. Yous is marryin' der whole feckin' family. An' dey'll have de shirt off yous back and de skin soon a'ter as soon as she's got her toight little erse in yous bed. Yous see if oi ain't feckin' roight.'

Kearney had been too busy drooling over the girl's Michelangelo-sculpted body and mile-high cheekbones to take proper note of what anyone else thought. So consumed with her was he that he'd even turned a blind eye to his wife's 'cousins' appearing from nowhere and taking over the kitchen to chew *miraa*, the local name for the narcotic *qat* plant, while she hacked at the remains of the goat they'd slaughtered in the bathroom.

'Well, at least it wasn't the bedroom,' he'd thought charitably on inquiring how long his 'guests' intended to stay. Through the fuzz of the narcotic stuffed in their cheeks, the cousins had just gazed at him with eyes incapable of looking in the same direction and Kearney had considered further inquiry an unprofitable waste of breath.

There was about as much explanation when Kearney came back from another safari to find his extended family had outgrown the house and spilled out into the garden, much to the gardener's disgust. From a lowly Kenyan tribe he might have been but to indigenous Kenyans no one was as lowly – or as despised – as the Somalis and to have them camped all over his preciously-tended lawn was more than the man could take. He'd only stayed on after Kearney promised to one day make him a safari guide. But even the prospect of leaping several rungs up the career ladder couldn't hold him on discovering goat blood smeared all over the hedge clippers.

The gardener's departure was met with a shrug of dismissal from Kearney's beloved.

'Who need gardener when have goats?' was her monosyllabic response as she scraped rebellious hairs from her clitoris-deprived crotch with his favourite razor.

Bedazzled by the girl's perfection, the issue of female circumcision had never entered Kearney's addled brain on proposing to her through the girl's father, the Kenya end of a thriving export business to Somalia. Coming from a family who'd been resident in one of Nairobi's better suburbs for the better part of three decades, Kearney never suspected he'd be marrying into a family clinging to the tradition of slashing their womenfolk's genitalia to ribbons.

On the wedding night, he was to have the scales of red mist rudely removed from his retinas. No touching, she'd commanded with a look of menace in her eyes when he'd tried.

'Eh? Why?' wailed the Somali's lovelorn husband.

He never got a reason, just his wife's assurance that 'jigjig ok enough. Be happy. I do all.'

If 'all' meant being content with nothing but the missionary position and getting to it without any preliminaries, then yes, he should be happy. He had a wife with the body of a goddess, all the basic penetration he could ever want and all without having to worry if he was satisfying her sexual needs. That, she'd made perfectly clear, was not an issue.

Somehow though, full, unadulterated marital bliss eluded him and as the weeks of married life turned to months Kearney found himself fantasising what her breasts, also off the menu, and crotch actually felt like and how her hand and mouth would feel on the shaft he'd taken to caressing in the shower. Despite all his pleadings, the only physical contact between them had been between his erection and the almost inanimate channel it was allowed to enter. Try anything else, he'd been warned, and he'd have her cousins to answer to.

The fact that they were camped outside his bedroom window in camel skin bivouacs sharpening an impressive collection of *panga* machetes not only focussed Kearney's mind wonderfully but inspired full compliance and further reinforced the reappraisal he was having about the family he'd married into.

Thinking back on it, maybe he had missed the odd sign or two that the family hadn't embraced the modern world with quite the degree of enthusiasm he'd assumed. Little things like the fact that his father-in-law's business consisted almost entirely of exporting *miraa* to Somalia and importing bush meat for Kenya's Somali community should perhaps have flagged the odd warning sign that the family was more tied to tradition than he'd led himself to believe.

As the realisation struck, it gave birth to a second that almost floored the first.

'Jaysus,' he exclaimed to himself, 'this is almost as bad as fockin' Ireland.'

* * *

The parallels were so close he wondered why he hadn't seen them before. Families apparently seeing no contradiction in imposing strict sexual mores on their offspring while dealing in drugs were the norm, not the exception, on the estates of his home town. There was only one real difference. Unlike the Catholic Irish, the Somalis had no need of confession. Without Rome and guilt there was nothing to confess.

'Well at least yous got dat goin' fer yous,' said Ryan on being made privy to Kearney's news that he'd had to pretend to become Moslem in order to marry the object of his desire.

'An' all yous has ter do ter be cert'n of a place in paradise is ter wait until yous old and infirm den blow yous self up takin' an infidel or two wid you. Solves two problems in one when yous tink about it. Yous avoids both hell and der care home at one and der same time… not dat der's a heap o' feckin' diff'rence.'

'Jaysus,' replied Kearney, 'fockin' explosives.' His whole life seemed to have revolved around them. First it was the Troubles on his own doorstep. Then it was his work with the oil crew where he'd had to fire them off to send shockwaves into the ground to see if there were any likely oil-bearing structures below. Now, if he wanted to go to paradise, he'd have to blow his own balls off.

The mere thought of it made him shudder. Not only did he have a fond attachment to them, but after a life of being exposed to loud bangs even fireworks sent him into a cold sweat these days.

The only consolation was that his time for being required to become a human Roman candle was still some way off and hopefully by then some enlightened imam or other might have managed to persuade his fellow Moslems that, actually, all life is sacred and that the taking of another's not only didn't guarantee a one-way trip to paradise but quite the opposite.

It was a forlorn hope, he knew that, and Ryan was minded to agree. Which was why he'd proposed that Kearney draw up a contingency plan in case his friend's sacrifice not only became inevitable but was brought forward for any reason.

'Yous never know,' he'd said to the now secretly-drinking Kearney. 'If dey gets any notion dat yous is Irishin' up yous orange juice wid vodka, yous moight foind yous name bein' pushed up der paradise trip list… as an act of atonement, so ter speak.'

The thought left Kearney without a proper night's sleep for weeks. Even if it had been made in jest, it had had the effect of bringing him back to reality with a thump. If he ever wanted to have a conscience-free drink, proper sex or see his lawn again, this madness had to stop.

But how? With divorce and disappearance both out of the question – his adopted family's response to either would make the donning of a suicide vest look like leniency – he'd have to find another way.

For days he wracked his brain. But with nothing coming immediately to mind, he decided the only way for inspiration to strike was to take himself off into the desert to think.

None the wiser a week later, he began the long, depressing trip home on the verge of simply accepting his fate only to discover that his family had solved the problem for him.

Finding them gone with everything he possessed, Kearney had breathed out for the first time in months. Partially, at least. While the threat of one Damoclesian sword hanging over him had been lifted, it'd been replaced by another. He still had to suffer Ryan's told-you-so face on acquainting him with the news that he'd won his bet.

In the end it wasn't as bad as he'd expected. Ryan did nothing but rub his hands together at the prospect of free, expensive drinks all night and Kearney was only too glad to oblige. Now, at least, he could get on with the rest of his life, one which he vowed would never ever see another bloody African woman in it.

chapter thirteen

Oooookay, thought Kearney as he fiddled with various electrical connections under the Falcon's hood. That vow was then, almost a decade ago, and until tonight he'd remained faithful to it. In all that time he'd not succumbed to any sort of African female temptation, even when tribal custom virtually demanded it.

The difference between that time a couple of weeks earlier and tonight was the drink. All he'd been offered by the stone age Turkana tribe chief he'd found himself supping with was milk and blood and he'd only agreed to drink that because he thought it would help win the old man's blessing to let his safari party camp in the tribe's territory.

If he'd gone the extra mile and accepted the offer of the use of a daughter or two, that blessing would have been given. But by declining on the spurious grounds that he had a bad stomach Kearney had been told to his face that he'd insulted the tribe and was therefore not worth doing business with. Whether it was the turning down of the daughter offer or, through the bad stomach excuse, the casting of aspersions on the tribe's version of gin and tonic that had made him *persona non grata*, Kearney knew not.

It didn't matter. Either way, through having to resort to taking the gaggle of Chinese tourists he'd reluctantly agreed to nursemaid on safari to the north Kenya badlands to a local hotel, it had led to Kearney losing money and to him cursing himself for having made the stupid African female intimacy avoidance vow in the first place.

After the events of the past few hours he was cursing himself again, this time for a very different reason.

How could he have been so fockin' stupid? Beatrice Kinyui was hot for it, of that there was no doubt. But doing it not only with another African woman but a married one at that, if that wasn't asking for trouble then he didn't know the meaning of the word. If her husband ever found out, they'd probably both end up going the same way as Robert Ouko, a former Kenyan foreign minister whose body had been discovered half-cremated in the Maasai Mara a couple of decades earlier after apparently killing himself and then, miraculously, setting himself on fire – or so the coroner's report had concluded.

While questions still hung over Ouko's death there'd be none if Kinyui's remains and his were discovered in the bush apparently the victims of an attack by lions armed with chainsaws. The judiciary was very clear on the law as it applied to the sullying of a Kenyan man's honour. There was no law.

So now Kearney had one more problem to add to a rather impressive list. If he ever got any inkling that he and Beatrice Kinyui had been rumbled it'd mean not one but a pair of tickets not only out of Kenya but out of Africa itself. Nowhere on the continent would escape the husband's scrutiny and Kearney would have to get them both off it to a place of comparative safety.

Somewhere like Syria, Kearney thought. True, they might fall victim to the barbaric Islamists running riot in those parts but it was still preferable to hiding out in Ireland. The treatment they could expect at the hands of fundamentalist fruitcakes would be nothing compared to the welcome his home town would give him on being confronted by a man of mixed faith turning up after nearly thirty years apparently intent on rubbing their noses in it by adding mixed race to the equation.

So no, Ireland would be out of the question, one that tomorrow, in the cold light of sobriety, he'd begin giving serious thought to.

'If there is a tomorrow,' he'd thought ruefully, glimpsing a set of lights bearing down on him in the distance. If they turned out to belong to the gang of thieving, murdering thugs who prowled these parts on moonless nights in search of drunken *mzungus* with cars worth stealing, tomorrow for Kearney could very well be cancelled.

As the lights closed in, Kearney felt his throat grow tighter than his grip on the flashlight, the only form of weapon he allowed himself in instances like this. Knowing there'd be too many of them to tackle on his own, the defence strategy he'd developed for such situations was genius personified though he said so himself.

While shining the light up under his chin would hardly be enough to scare them off, it might at least add an element of levity to the situation and no laughing attacker, he'd done his best to convince himself, ever got seriously violent. The hope was that the jest might just be enough to persuade them to take pity on him and simply leave him vehicle-less and abandoned in the middle of nowhere.

It might, but only if he could get the old bitch's lights working. Finding they were stealing a car they couldn't drive, they might not be quite so understanding.

* * *

The closer the lights got, the more Kearney felt his body brace. But then a new sensation took over. Kearney felt his brow creasing into a quizzical, bemused frown as the oncoming vehicle came within earshot. If it did contain a gang of marauding, murdering scum, they were the noisiest gang of marauding, murdering scum he'd come across in all his years in Africa.

No hoodlum worth his salt ever made that sort of racket. Like lions, they crept silently up on you, gathered themselves for the kill then pounced. If this one contained carjackers, they were either new to the job or celebrating an already successful evening's blag.

Either way, the mobile din rapidly bearing down on him gave Kearney heart. If they were new boys, there was a chance they'd be more likely to fall for his flashlight stunt than their veteran counterparts.

Even better, if it was a gang celebrating an earlier success they could well decide to ignore him altogether and roar past into the night.

They didn't. Screeching to a halt in a cloud of dust in the off-road dirt behind the Falcon, the only thing the shrieking occupants of the incoming *matatu* minibus did ignore was his flashlight stunt.

Disgorged from the *matatu*, sound system giving the big bang a run for its money, the vehicle's complete complement of passengers charged at him Zulu warrior style... and straight past him to descend on his vehicle like a pack of hyenas on the corpse of a freshly-butchered wildebeest.

With Kearney standing stock still in the dust, flashlight shining up under his chin, a hundred fingers and thumbs tore at any electrical connection they could find, their owners bickering like dogs over whose remedy was best.

Moments later, the Falcon's lights blazed again, thirty grinning Africans leapt back in their *matatu* and roared off up the Ngong Road swerving and honking and leaving a wide-eyed Kearney standing next to the Falcon feeling both bemused and a tad stupid. They'd swooped in like Superman, done the job in seconds and taken off without a word of explanation, hardly noticing the horror face impersonation he was doing in the glare of his flashlight. Something, he suddenly realised, he was still doing.

As they disappeared, Kearney found himself wondering how the events of the past sixty seconds would have looked to an innocent bystander.

Something like a guerrilla performance art stunt probably. There was about as much rhyme or reason to it, all of which left Kearney staring into the night and wondering if the drink and the worry had got the better of him.

It took two days for evidence to emerge that they hadn't.

During a trip to Ngong Town to get a tyre repaired, the repair man had asked him how the Falcon was running.

The question surprised Kearney. No African had ever asked him that before. All they ever cared about was whether the owner might consider parting with his vehicle for half what it was worth. So why the deviation now?

It took a while for the penny to drop. Staring at the man, Kearney suddenly realised he was in the presence of one of his roadside helpers. One, the man told him, who'd been part of an Ngong mechanics' night out to Nairobi that'd been curtailed early on receiving news of the wife of one of their number going into premature labour.

Kearney's jaw dropped. Nothing short of arrest or death or the football World Cup final, he knew, could keep an African man from the birth of what he prayed would be a son. So why had they stopped for him? Good Samaritan acts were virtually unheard of in carjack city lest breakdowns turn out to be set-ups.

'But that what we are, *bwana*,' said the man with a grin. 'We ourselves are members of Our Saviour's Church of Number One Good Samaritans. Helpers of peoples in distress and even Asians. Minister preaches us to follow Lord Jesus and save all from torment and damnation.'

The explanation left Kearney in emotional turmoil. While he knew he should be entertaining feelings of sincere, unconditional gratitude towards the man's church for sending the man and his fellow church devotees his way, it was something he just couldn't bring himself to express.

After a lifetime of exposure to religious hypocrisy and the zealots it had infected, Kearney didn't know which he despised more, churches like the one to which the man belonged or the people who allowed themselves to fall under their ministers' hypnotic, profiteering spells.

To a man who'd seen lives ruined by the church in all its forms, his friend's 'Jesus saved me from the fiery furnace' gushings left Kearney not just cold but wanting to vomit. He didn't, but only out of fear that to do so might leave him with a tyre unrepaired.

Instead, he managed to restrict himself to a fixed rictus grin, one he hoped would camouflage the avalanche of thoughts his friend might find a tad churlish and uncharitable under the circumstances.

It wasn't the message the churches preached that had Kearney frothing at the mouth. It was how these sellers of religious snake oil went about preaching it. If they just left it at 'be nice to one another', he wouldn't have had a problem. But threatening eternal damnation on those devoid of the wit to question the sales pitch and terrified by the prospect of being deprived of a life hereafter unless they kept the church's coffers filled to the brim, to Kearney that was simple extortion by an operation that could only be described as the Church of the Fly-by-Night Predator Feeding on the Souls of the Spiritually Simple-Minded.

In short, he thought, such 'churches' were nothing short of giant religious Ponzi schemes trapping the deprived, the impressionable and the desperate in their cynical web of deceit and doing very nicely out of it thank you.

A lot, Kearney thought, like the Catholic Church. Trading on the promulgation of paranoia and profiting handsomely from the sale of dubious remedies to those least able to afford them, the names of these new evangelist operations and Rome were interchangeable. Both were equally odious and left Kearney hoping with some degree of fervour that there really was a hell. If there wasn't, there'd be nowhere for these pedlars of perfidy to collect their just rewards.

Kearney's view of the followers of such dubious enterprises was only marginally more charitable. While not blaming the under-educated amongst them for falling under the spell of those selling the prospect of an escape from their Earthly hell, he did take exception to being seen as the vehicle for making that escape possible. Without exception, followers of these churches seemed to view the successful conversion of non-followers to their cause as air miles towards their tickets to eternal bliss and never stopped in their quest to swell their specific church's numbers. Each new pew seat filled represented another tick on the spiritual bingo card of the one who'd been responsible for filling it.

If Kearney had entertained any doubts about the true motivations behind the so-called Good Samaritans' acts of humanity, they were dispelled the day he was confronted by an epidemic of Jesusboards littering the country's roadsides.

'Follow Jesus!,' they screamed at passers-by. 'Save YOURSELF!'

Kearney took the instruction to heart. The second part anyway.

'Thanks,' he told them, 'I will.' Starting, he thought, with taking a leaf out of the book of an equally ardent religion-despising friend who'd found himself seated next to a happy-clapper on a long-haul flight from which there was no escape.

Knowing he'd have to nip the assault in the bud before it got going in earnest, in response to the inevitable 'Have you been born again?' inquiry, Kearney's friend had smiled a smile of sweet benevolence and responded with a reply that had won him twelve blissful hours of being totally ignored by the maniacal religious midwife sitting next to him.

'Not bloody likely,' he'd said. 'Once was enough.'

As much as he'd have liked to have treated his roadside helper to something equally as withering, prudence, Kearney decided, was definitely the better part of valour on this occasion. Right now, with Beatrice Kinyui's husband probably already on his trail, the last thing he needed was more enemies.

So no, Kearney told himself firmly, this was not the time to alienate his new 'friend'. Quite the opposite in fact. After all, since the mission of the man's church was to pull people out of holes, maybe those holes extended beyond the provision of roadside assistance to the involuntary hole dweller.

If they did, Kearney found himself fantasising, who knew? It might even encompass the conjuring up of miracles, the kind Kearney knew he was going to need to make the Kinyui problem go away. Now, if they could just do that, he'd not only be prepared to consider overlooking this Church of the Latter Day Pickpocket's more heinous crimes but joining up himself.

Kearney was pretty confident it'd never come to that. Apart from the almost one hundred percent certainty that miracles weren't within the church's standard remit, once they'd been appraised of the reason why he needed a miracle it seemed unlikely they'd consider having him as one of their number even if he nailed himself to the neon cross that lit up the tin shack masquerading as their House of God. Helping an adulterer escape divine retribution for breaking one of the bible's cardinal rules might not be to their advantage when it came to achieving everlasting bliss.

So no, when it came to dealing with the upshot of word concerning his and Beatrice Kinyui's activities in the back of the Falcon reaching the ears of Mr Kinyui, Kearney knew he'd be on his own and that his top priority was to second guess where that word might leak from and plug it before it did.

The more he thought about it, the longer the list of potential leak sources got. Trying to put generosity aside and focus on reality, the list read from the top:

– Beatrice Kinyui herself who, as much as he tried to persuade himself otherwise, might just decide to pre-empt any leak and throw herself on the mercy of her husband in an attempt to save her own skin;

– Ryan, whose lips could never be trusted, especially when they'd been round a bottle;

– The Pratt twat who might just be vindictive enough to put them in the frame for undermining his academic dignity;

– The party's host who'd looked quizzically at them as they'd left the party together without saying goodbye;

– Any number of others who might have been sober enough to note their joint progress out of the hotel;

– The hotel doorman who'd smiled knowingly at Kearney and then at the receptionist as they passed;

– A couple arguing in the car park over who had the keys;

– And last, but most certainly not least, that bloody *askari*.

In short, if you added in all the hotel residents who might have been looking out of their windows at the very moment he and Beatrice threw themselves inside the Falcon like a pair of sex-starved monkeys, there were hundreds of possibilities.

All it needed was one to start a rumour. One that, in a city where gossip beat even drinking as the national pastime, would in days find itself converted to solid, indisputable, written-in-blood fact and come home to roost like the metaphorical vultures that had appeared from nowhere to start doing their circular, psychic, dinner-is-about-to-be-served death dance directly above his head.

chapter fourteen

Vultures, although he didn't know it at the time, were the least of Kearney's worries. They at least had the decency to wait until their dinner was dispatched, disembowelled and decomposing before arriving in force. No such courtesy with the bird of prey that had Kearney in its sights and was going in for the kill.

'You'll never believe this, Gideon, but the Irishman is actually trying to blackmail me,' the bird of prey reported to her 'employer' a few days after the party. 'ME! Beatrice Kinyui!'

'Well, he's got balls, I'll say that for him,' said Kariuki. 'I rather suspected he had after that attempt to tap me up for a loan. Seems the man just doesn't know his limitations. I like that. It shows tenacity.'

'Or basic stupidity,' countered Kinyui. 'You'd have thought he'd have done some basic research on the person he intended to put the screws on before actually doing it.'

'D'you think that'd have stopped him? I'd say he's desperate enough to try anything given what you've told me.'

As expected, Kinyui had reported to Kariuki, Kearney had materialised on her workplace doorstep some days after the party but not with the expected intent. Rather than tracking her down to deliver a doleful lovelorn plea to be allowed to keep seeing her, he'd come with an offer his manner indicated he felt she couldn't refuse.

'The insolent man actually had the audacity to believe I'd be willing to pay for his silence *a propos* the Landrover incident! The little shit all but threatened me with letting word slip within earshot of my husband unless I agreed to help him out with something. The BASTARD! Thinking I'd go for something so… prehistoric. The man is clearly living in the dark ages!'

'So what was it he wanted?'

'A name. One he said he knew I was in a position to provide. After that, and I quote, I'd be "free to walk the streets safe in the knowledge that should your husband ever get to hear of the incident, that information would not be coming from me."'

'What name?'

'Eh? Oh… one of the KWS officials. The one in charge of the country's confiscated wildlife body parts stockpile.'

'How very interesting. The man's mind is more difficult to read than I thought. Surely he can't be thinking of doing what I think he's thinking of doing. Can you get it?'

'Of course. That's one thing the bloody man hasn't missed. If anyone knows the name, it's someone with access to the Kenya Wildlife Service's human resources data.'

* * *

A week after 'the incident', as Kearney had put it to Kinyui, the vultures in Kearney's head had started looking elsewhere for their dinner and Kearney had just about started breathing again. Not only had there been no repercussions but he hadn't even noticed the odd, meaningful glance in his direction from people he knew to be the biggest vultures of all.

He didn't even have Ryan to worry about. A few days after the party, the man had absented himself from the capital, taking off for Bushwacker Camp to fill in for the camp's regular mechanic who'd come off second best to a baboon he'd discovered taking a shit on his bed.

So it was with some relief that Kearney sat down to plan his next great money-making venture. One he was certain this time had no chance of failure since, for once, Kearney had built a series of fail-safe valves into a plan whose kernel was planted way back in those dark days of having to share his house with half the Somali nation.

Faced with an electricity bill of jaw dropping proportions after his in-laws had abandoned their traditional practice of drying bush meat in the sun in favour of hanging it in front of his air conditioners turned to heat mode at the height of Kenya's hottest season, Kearney had had no option but to come up with a power-saving scheme to avoid a rapid slide into bankruptcy.

If the in-laws weren't going to use the sun, he'd decided, maybe he should. For some time he'd been toying with the idea of going solar and now, he thought, might be the time. A substantial stock of solar panels and batteries had come to his attention gathering dust in an aid agency compound after one of its projects went south and it seemed a shame to let them go to waste.

So, with the help of the Millennium Falcon, a borrowed low-loader and the collusion of the aid agency's Kenyan manager, Kearney was soon in possession of a solar system that'd have cost him ten times what he'd paid if he'd had to source it on the open market.

Kearney smiled inwardly for several reasons as the next batch of bush meat was hung up in front of his newly solar-powered air conditioner. Without knowing it, his in-laws had failed to fully abandon their traditional sun-drying habits, he'd helped an aid agency put abandoned equipment to good use and the only one losing out on the deal was the American insurance company that was now in receipt of the aid agency's insurance claim. It had a curiously satisfying ring to it.

The smile lasted right up to the Irishman's return from his next safari gig. Swanning in through his compound gates, Kearney had been greeted by a battalion of fuming in-laws, a colony of flies in permanent residence in his living room, an empty space where the batteries had been and a smirking neighbour caressing an ancient Toyota Landcruiser, all but abandoned in the neighbour's driveway for want of the funds to replace its long since demised battery.

Unable to report the theft to the police – as the neighbour knew full well – Kearney had had no option but to reconnect the air conditioners to the mains and wrack his brain for an alternative to the battery storage problem. Replacing the missing ones with new would once again put him in bankruptcy territory.

It was just the motivation he needed to finally alight on a money-making brainwave that this time he was certain could simply not go wrong. What was needed was a technology that couldn't be removed without some serious heavy-lifting equipment and Kearney thought he knew the very thing. While gathering up the batteries and solar panels, he'd spotted a heavy duty air compressor and a collection of gas bottles cluttering up the aid agency's project equipment depot. Without a disproportionate amount of effort, the compressor could be made to substitute for the batteries.

Within the week the machine was humming contentedly away in Kearney's garden shed, the aid agency compound watchman was paying for a new identity card and drinks all round in a north Kenya badlands bar out of a roll of shilling bills big enough to burst his trouser pocket and the aid agency chief, as Kearney knew he would, had succumbed to his conscience over whether to subject the watchman to Kenya's dehumanising prison conditions.

Once all the groundwork had been laid, Kearney had accomplished the relocation singlehanded in just a few night hours and this time his neighbour would be none the wiser.

Out of sight and under lock and key in the garden shed, the compressor was doing exactly what Kearney wanted it to do.

Powered by the solar panels by day, the machine steadily compressed air into the gas bottles, releasing it at night to drive a small turbine generator connected to the air conditioners thus ensuring full day/night operation and the full contentment of his extended family.

It was that contentment that prompted the Kearney brainwave. Seeing how it changed the lives of his relatives, Kearney woke one night punching the air with enlightenment. If his diehard traditionalist in-laws could take to the system with such aplomb, there seemed no reason why every electricity-deprived village in Africa shouldn't do likewise and by morning Kearney had the guts of a scheme for replicating the technology the length and breadth of the continent mapped out on the back of a scrap of solar-dried goat skin. Somehow it seemed fitting.

* * *

Whittled down to its bare bones, the scheme centred on doing something the aid agencies should have been doing but, for reasons best known to them, weren't. What seemed crystal clear to Kearney – but despite all the evidence, not to the aid agencies – was that it wasn't technology the deprived African needed but the product of that technology. The average African could never afford a complete solar system. But once he'd seen what such a system could do would very likely sign up to pay for its power output in modest instalments.

It was a brainwave that'd been inspired by one of the most ludicrous aid projects Kearney had come across in all his years in Africa. One of the UN's agencies, he discovered, was pumping millions of scarce resources into a solar-powered radio scheme that could only have been dreamed up in the plush environs of one of the better restaurants surrounding the agency's head office.

The agency, Kearney's investigations revealed, was paying a major multinational millions to design a radio containing an inbuilt solar cell that was supposed to displace the need for batteries. Not only that, but the best brains in the UN had decided that, to recoup the design cost outlay, the radio would have to be sold at a cost equivalent to about a year of the average African's labour in the fields of his robber baron landlord.

Once Kearney had recovered the power of speech on being made privy to the details of the scheme, rage hardly covered his reaction.

'The fockin' stupid bastards! Don't they know your average African already has a fockin' radio. What he doesn't have is the power to fockin' run it. And he's certainly not going to fork out on a radio that doesn't even have shortwave. That's the one thing he might be prepared to invest in to get an alternative to the incessant government FM propaganda!'

The more Kearney fumed, the more idiotic the project looked and the more brilliant his own became. Not only would subscribers to his scheme be getting regular power whether the sun shone or not, but they'd be getting it for just a few hundred shillings a month. What was not to like?

The more he thought about it, the wider his grin got. Once the initial capital cost had been covered the rest would be almost pure profit AND he'd be able to sleep at night. Not only did zero fossil fuel use mean negligible running costs but, after a lifetime helping pollute the planet with both his oil exploration expertise and his devotion to the Millennium Falcon's gas-guzzling engine, his place on the environmental honours board looked assured. It was, in the words of Stevie Marriott, all too beautiful and Kearney's head was wreathed in smiles as it hit the pillow that night next to that of his dearly beloved's apparently intent on snoring itself resolutely off.

* * *

The smile lasted all of a week – right up to the moment he returned from his sojourn in the desert to ponder a means of escape from the clutches of his in-laws.

Pulling onto the dirt track that led to his house, something told him that his old friend Mwangi had made a visit in his absence. Normally friendly neighbours ignored his wave, shoo-ing their children indoors as he passed. Women working on their *shamba*s stopped their hoe-ing and stared at him through unsmiling death masks. Even the regular riot of dogs, cats and chickens stopped in mid-riot and fell silent. It was as if someone had grassed him up as a government assassin. Or worse, a mercenary in the pay of the collector of taxes.

As he rounded the bend leading to his house, the real reason became clear. Gate wide open, no *askari* to salute his return, all bushes cleared of their usual foliage of drying clothes, all goats and Somali bivouacs gone from the garden, no wife or extended family ignoring his entrance and, worst of all, no solar panels on the roof or air compressor in the shed that wasn't there.

Frozen-faced and wide-eyed with surprise, Kearney slewed to a halt in front of the house and stared around to check he was in the right compound.

He was. The greasy baseball cap he wore when working on the Falcon left lying on the floor beneath the missing hook it normally hung on confirmed it. Not even his thieving in-laws wanted that.

Or maybe they'd overlooked it… unlike absolutely everything else that wasn't fixed in place with bolts of tensile steel. Not a door or window or light fitting had escaped their attention and even the toilets were gone although what they could possibly want with them he couldn't imagine. It wasn't as if they'd ever bothered to learn how to flush them.

Shuffling speechless from doorless room to doorless room to assess the carnage one thing became immediately clear. Mwangi had definitely been here, rendering the house uninhabitable save to the feral cat that hissed menacingly at him from the place the kitchen sink had once been, now replaced by a litter of evil-looking kittens busily tearing a sizeable cobra to shreds.

Less clear was Kearney's feelings on the matter. On the one hand his world had been turned upside down, on the other he knew that any tears of remorse would be of the crocodile variety.

Suddenly single and homeless again, he felt unloved, abandoned and betrayed and, as if that wasn't enough, he'd not only been relieved of the fabric of his money-making dream but was facing a substantial repairs bill from Shylock the landlord unless he could restore the house to its former glory before the old miser's next due visit in a couple of weeks time.

But at least his in-laws had saved him the trouble of doing a runner himself, the only remedy for the situation he'd got himself into he could think of. And they'd quit the premises without getting their greasy goat herding hands on his pride and joy. With the Falcon parked right outside, engine still hot from his safari, roof rack stacked full of all the equipment he'd need to set up camp in his own front yard, all in all, things didn't look as black as at first sight and Kearney even felt a small smile of contentment cross his lips, a smile that even Ryan's sniggering smirk of triumph failed to fully dislodge.

* * *

Kearney and Ryan's paths hadn't crossed since Kearney had had his solar-powered compressed air energy storage epiphany. Being under the thumb of a wife with a tendency for dispatching male relatives to intercept him at the first hint of any falling back into old habits not only made meeting up with Ryan a problem but had put Ryan himself off the idea.

Never one to wholeheartedly endorse Kearney's choice of bride, the man from Cork had all but decided that his and Kearney's partnership should be put on ice until Kearney came to his senses… or had them restored to him by the reality of sharing his house with a tribe of opportunistic savages.

Until that time inevitably came, Ryan had turned his attentions elsewhere, preferring the company of like-minded recidivists, deviants and general goodtime grifters who lived their lives by the rule of taking full advantage of polite society's trusting nature to keep their pockets filled with the proceeds of dubious exploits.

In Ryan's case, when not distressing ostrich bones in Kenya's scorched earth and passing them off to tourists as the bones of ancient raptorsaurs, the man was to be found either at the Nairobi racecourse using his Irishness to convince chinless punters that he was a fount of knowledge on all things horsey, filling in for other dipsomaniac mechanics until their DT's had cleared or overseeing prestigious construction projects for householders persuaded of the sense of paying just a little more for the skills of an Irish-born master builder.

'Tis common knowledge,' went Ryan's self-promoting blarney, 'dat when it comes to der buildin' werk, no one has der touch of der Paddy. If yous wants a ting done roight, bring in de Oirish. Everyone knows dat.'

When it worked – and when prospective clients could make out what Ryan was saying – it worked like a dream. Ryan sub-contracted the job to a local man anyway, made a great show of supervising him and his gang, paid the gang the local rate for the job and sat back out of the dehydrating sun counting the money.

Then, in the recognised manner of his forebears, he spent it all on drink, gambling and whoring and started all over again.

To Ryan it was just the way the universe was arranged and he had no great desire, nor the wit, to rock the boat of the natural order of things.

That said, if the main chance ever did present itself he was realistic to know two things. He wouldn't be averse to grasping it and that that chance wouldn't be coming from him. That was most definitely Kearney's department and Ryan couldn't wait for the day the man sloped sheepishly into the bar with his tail between his legs and the news that at last he'd seen the light.

When that day finally arrived, barely eleven months into the Kearney marriage experiment, Ryan could scarcely contain himself, jumping up from the table in one of Voi's less savoury establishments to all but embrace his erstwhile partner. It wasn't just that he was pleased to see him, it was that his plan to fleece a bunch of humble local railway workers at Bourré wasn't going exactly according to plan. Despite their head scratching when he'd outlined the rules of the evil poker/whist crossover game to them, they'd proved rather more adept at it than he'd expected leaving Ryan himself looking for a way to leave the table with his shirt still on his back.

Listening to Kearney's homecoming experience with a smile that grew exponentially wider with every facet of the burgeoning tale of betrayal, he was almost laughing out loud by the time Kearney got to the part about the disappearance of the solar panels and the air compressor.

At which point Ryan's smile froze. Ryan hadn't needed much persuasion to recognise the money-making potential of the concept, one that wasn't just Kearney's ticket out of Africa. It was his too and its theft – which could hardly be reported to the police – left the pair without a prototype to demonstrate to potential project backers. Now they'd have to raise the funds to start all over again. It wasn't every day you came across failing aid projects involving the use of solar technologies run by a manager who was prepared to bend the rules a little and the pair weren't blind to the likelihood of having to actually shell out real money if they wanted to get back to square one.

Since raising it at the Bourré table was looking unlikely, Ryan's marked men playing on without him as he listened to Kearney's story and demonstrating a surprising level of acumen for a game they claimed to be playing for the first time, the pair first looked at one another, then at the ceiling and finally into their respective bottles for inspiration. With none forthcoming in any place their eyes alighted, they finally gave in and did what they always did in situations like this. They got drunk and waited for inspiration to find them.

*   *   *

After getting short shrift and directions to the way out from every aid agency and bank they could think of approaching for the funds to get the scheme going, Kearney's brainwave looked dead in the water and the pair were forced to concede that if they were ever to bring the system to market they'd have to look elsewhere for the funds.

Hard as they tried, as the years rolled by with everyone they approached reacting in much the same way as the banks and aid agencies, that elsewhere began to look as distant as the hallowed turf of their precious Galway racetrack.

But then had come Moses, the Chinese and Beatrice Kinyui and the dream of lifting a pint in a west of Ireland rain-battered pub while toasting their great escape and warming their backsides over the pub's roaring peat fire lived again. Just a few more ducks and dives along the road and the pair would be back in the auld sod grinning like loons as they listened to old Paddy's interminable tales of an Ireland long gone while calculating how much each second of each tale was bringing them in solar electricity sales to Africa's newly powered-up village dwellers.

chapter fifteen

Thinking back on the day he discovered what Xinhua had in mind for him, Xi wondered if you were born with the level of malevolence his former editor had shown or if it was the unavoidable evolutionary end-product of Chinese state systemisation.

'The latter,' Xi's inner voice told him, 'definitely the latter' and Xi was minded to agree. When there was no one else to turn to for advice or wise counsel Xi knew better than to argue. Anyway, the evidence was all there. Xi just needed it pointed out to him.

'You know as well as I do that elevation to high office and abuse of the system are directly proportional,' said the voice. 'Considering your own experience, you don't need me to tell you that the higher the Party official climbs the further he gets from the communist ethos. Every step up the ladder takes him closer to utter disdain for his "comrades", a word that's come to mean "the lower order riffraff" up at the highest levels.

'T'was ever thus and you know it,' said the voice. 'Even in Mao's day the Party high-ups played fast and loose with the system. It's all there on the internet. No wonder the state's spending so much time and effort trying to control it. The last thing they want is news getting out that our revered leaders aren't above treating their status as passports for abusing their positions.

'So I don't know how you could find the editor's actions surprising when both he and you found yourselves in the same orbit during those days of peak system abuse. You were always going to end up with the shit end of the stick.'

'Yeah,' agreed Xi. 'When you put it like that, it was inevitable. Power, pride and money. That's what it was all about back then. Not that things have changed much.'

The only real difference between then and now, Xi found himself reflecting, was that it was all so new to China during his first years at Xinhua. Even though Mao had died twenty years earlier and his successor Deng Xiaoping had opened China's doors to the rest of the world, what was rapidly becoming the world's factory was still grappling with the concept of being a fledgling economic superpower.

Well, some were grappling with it. Others got it a lot quicker than others and were swift to spot the hay-making potential of China's new status. Result – rampant corruption, abuse of power and people like Xi's editor.

The man typified the genre of elevated Chinese official who'd grasped how important the country was becoming to the global economy and weren't backward in taking full advantage of it. Bloated egos blossomed in the offices of officials who considered themselves instrumental in putting China's name back on the map, egos that built to full-blown megalomania when the country could finally claim to have gained access to the world powers club.

In Xi's first year at the state news agency it rapidly became clear to him that China's policy of reconnecting with the world centred almost exclusively on making itself an indispensible part of the global manufacturing base. Of undercutting everyone else in order to make the West in particular a hopeless addict of Chinese-made products. That much was clear from reading between the lines of the stories that crossed his desk.

As the turn of the millennium loomed it was equally clear that that addiction had all but been accomplished and that China was ready to launch its follow-up plan. Now, the leaders were saying without saying it, it was time to remind the rest of the world of

China's history. To let them know in no uncertain terms that a country able to trace its civilisation three millennia further back than anyone else's would no longer tolerate being treated like the caterer at meetings of the world's major players.

Everything was now geared to delivering the message and, in 2001, China finally got a reply. Unable to ignore the dragon on its doorstep any longer, the rest of the world had not only caved-in to Chinese pressure to be allowed to join the World Trade Organisation but had deemed Beijing fit to host the 2008 Olympics.

Unconstrained joy and celebration hardly described China's reaction to the news. Now, at last, the country's high officials could show up at world power gatherings without being greeted with 'what are THEY doing here?' mutterings from the other participants.

The news, as Xi was only too aware from his vantage point at the heart of China's propaganda machine, sent the machine into overdrive. It was as if Xinhua hadn't really appreciated before how far it could go with self-glorification. Nothing escaped being given the Chinese chest-thump treatment. Nothing was beyond being dressed up in gold leaf to shout the Motherland's name from the pagoda tops, even when the country was hit by the debilitating Severe Acute Respiratory Syndrome and half the country was put into isolation.

When SARS struck in 2003, Xi recognised Xinhua's response as classic China. The agency turned bad news into good by focussing on nothing but how China had mobilised its glorious medical research teams to lick a problem that had the rest of the world stumped.

Despite the gradually emptying work cubicles as SARS raged through the Xinhua workforce, Xi almost began believing it himself. With China's newfound confidence in itself being as infectious as the virus that was ripping the country apart, Xi found himself swept away on the tide of self-adulation. Spurred ever onwards by those at China's top table, Xi and those of his colleagues who'd escaped infection found themselves churning out the good news while doing the work of three to please an editor determined that nothing but pure gold got relayed to the rest of the world.

Xi wasn't surprised at the editor's diktat. Not only did he have a neck to protect but a job that was the envy of Chinese journalism. In the wake of the WTO and Olympics announcements, China had effectively been given carte blanche to strut its own stuff by the rest of the world and those with the power to do so had handed responsibility for ensuring it was well-strutted to Xinhua's big dog. End product – a man bordering on clinical psychosis overlording an army of ten thousand workers left in no doubt as to who was who in the Xinhua firmament.

As the years passed, the editor's power craze grew in direct proportion to China's belief in itself and, by the time Xi received his 'invite' to the twenty-first floor, the mania had not only completely consumed him but had transmuted into a scarcely-veiled streak of pure malice. Xi had only needed to be in the man's company twice to discover how malicious. Leaving the office after his second visit it was abundantly clear to Xi that the Xinhua staff's pain was the editor's sadistic gain.

Even so, looking back on it in the aftermath of the event Xi still hadn't really understood why the location-withholding charade had been necessary at all. The editor could simply have ordered him to pack his bags and board the plane to Africa. Who was he to argue?

But that was before he knew what he knew now. Before he knew that the editor had had to play the game in the way he had if he was to accomplish a tricky task while not allowing a deep-seated malevolence to go unsatisfied. By acting as he had, he'd not only filled a difficult post but had made an underling squirm with uncertainty at one and the same time.

* * *

Looking back, Xi was almost tempted to applaud the editor's cunning. The man had clearly learned a thing or two in his time, not least how to entice unwilling parties to do his bidding. In this case, to sign up for a posting to the one overseas Xinhua bureau no one volunteered for.

With China riding the wave of newfound global influence, new Xinhua bureaux were being opened up across the world and while there was no shortage of staff vying to fill the plum jobs in New York, London and Paris, in Africa the editor knew that if he relied on volunteers alone, the editorial contingent was likely to be outnumbered by the cleaning staff.

Africa's reputation for savagery, thuggery and general mayhem had not gone unnoticed by the Xinhua staff. They hadn't joined the agency to find themselves simmering in a cannibal's cooking pot, still the predominant image of Africa carried around in the heads of people like Xi even halfway through the first decade of the twenty-first century. Even in the coalfields Xi had heard stories of the ritualised disembowelling of Chinese workers going to help the development efforts of Maoist-orientated African countries. And from reports coming back it apparently wasn't unusual for wildlife-watchers to end up eviscerated by the beasts they'd come to watch if the beasts noticed so much as a slant-eyed look from their audience, something of a disadvantage for a Chinese.

So, all in all, Africa was not a popular destination for the Chinese which, Xi was now fully aware, gave both Xinhua and every other Chinese operation setting up there a problem. If they were to make inroads into the wide open opportunity that was Africa, they'd need to come up with a subtle strategy for encouraging Chinese workers to make the trip.

While some Chinese organisations used simple financial inducements, most resorted to rather more insidious means, Xinhua not excluded. The peddling of plain untruths to get people to sign up was commonplace, as was, in the most extreme cases, transportation.

In Xi's case, although Xi didn't know it at the time, the editor was utilising the last two in equal devious measure. By simply 'forgetting' to mention to Xi that his public service sentence had expired, Xi's dispatch to a place no one else would go was press ganging in all but name.

Looking back, Xi could imagine the editor sitting back and smiling at the irony of what had just transpired. Press ganging was a pretty apt description of what he'd trapped Xi into doing. He'd not only coerced a member of staff into accepting a news agency posting he had every right to refuse but had obtained Xi's signature on a note showing quite clearly that Xi had volunteered for the job.

If the editor ever found himself in a position of having to explain his actions, the note – an only marginally incomplete record of his meetings with Xi which Xi had been 'advised' to sign if he wanted to stay with Xinhua – was proof of Xi's compliancy. The editor had seen the 'volunteer' sign on the dotted line, so how was he to know his recruit had felt under obligation to accede to the 'request'?

chapter sixteen

If the editor had any qualms about finding himself pilloried for this bit of cheap chicanery, from what Xi now knew, he needn't have worried. Such sharp practice was not only regulation procedure amongst Chinese companies keen to capitalise on Africa's under-exploited potential but effectively had the government's unwritten seal of approval.

No one was more keen to see such companies on African soil than the country's leaders. Chinese firms were the spearhead of its policy for making friends on the continent and if a little coercion was needed to fill the positions opening up, who was it to complain? If it did, it might emerge that the state's own hands were hardly blemish-free. Certain government projects would never have seen the light of day had it not been for teams of ultra-willing, highly-skilled and motivated workers recruited from China's prisons.

It was something Xi knew only too well. But what he'd never suspected until much, much later was that he'd been 'recruited' under false pretences. So far as he was aware, he was still in debt to the state and going to Africa on Xinhua's behalf was just another in a long line of repayment instalments. So far as he was aware at the time, he had no alternative but to go to help China cement its place on a continent just crying out to be re-colonised.

Xi's research in the short time he was allowed before being packed off to Nairobi showed there was no other word for it. Ever since 1990 when the Berlin wall came down, the Cold War ended and the US and Russia stopped bickering over scraps of 'strategic' African territory, Africa had lain there like a defenceless child just waiting for some kind person to come along and advise it what to do with the fortune it was sitting on.

With the rest of the world passing by and looking the other way, China took it upon itself to take on the mantle of benevolent uncle, a bit like Europe did in the nineteenth century but with a tad more guile. Unlike Britain, France, Spain, Belgium and Portugal, China slipped in almost unnoticed with gifts the African child could hardly ignore.

'Here,' it said, 'please take these toys to play with' and while the child was reaching for the beguiling objects placed just beyond arm's length, China surreptitiously removed the golden cushion from beneath the child's bottom.

Although never put in quite that way in the files Xi unearthed in the Xinhua databank, you didn't need the university degree Xi had been deprived of to read between the lines of the official communiqués. Africa was a prime target for re-colonisation and the means of accomplishing it would have had Kearney and Ryan clinking glasses over getting that one so spot on. Xi's findings accorded almost precisely with what the Irish pair had witnessed taking place on the ground. About the only things that didn't were their respective levels of knowledge over the degree of respect held by the Chinese for the average African and Xi's knowledge that, for sure, China wasn't in Africa because of the Irish.

Being primarily drawn from official documents, Xi's research left him little option but to conclude that China's motives for being in Africa and its companies' regard for fellow members of the under-developed world were honourable. It wasn't until he'd been there a few months that the scales fell from his eyes and he could see what Kearney and Ryan had been seeing for years.

To China, it was clear that Africa was little more than a rich, relatively undefended untapped vein of all the things China needed to keep the wheels of industrial hyper-production turning and its leaders had adopted a relatively straightforward strategy for relieving Africa of its burdensome mineral wealth – bribery.

The upshot – Chinese envoys had begun descending on Africa's capitals bearing gifts. Gifts that took the form of re-paved roads, resurrected railways and revived ports. In short, all the things China would itself need to get the wealth out and relocated back to the Orient. And all it wanted in return was Africa's signature on a couple of documents, one giving China exclusive rights to virtually anything it could find and one pledging support for Beijing's One-China policy.

With these two signatures in its possession, China would be assured of not only maintaining an uninterrupted flow of raw materials in its direction but of adding yet another 'friend' to its list of countries backing China's campaign to re-unite the renegade Taiwan with the mainland. And just to show it meant what it said about the covenant being a mutually beneficial win-win arrangement, China pledged not to do what Africa's former colonisers had done – interfere.

'Sign here,' it said, 'and rest assured that we'll just get on with the business end of the arrangement leaving you free to do whatever it is you have to do to keep the country stable. If that means diverting some of the development money on offer into accounts not strictly related to the country's development, be assured that this government is not in the business of advising the governments of other countries how to run their affairs.'

At the time Xi was doing his research, although the policy was in its early stages of implementation it was bearing enough fruit to encourage both continuation and enhancement. China/Africa trade had grown from just one billion dollars in 1980 to forty times that in 2005 and Beijing had seen the transfer of African diplomatic allegiances from Taipei to the People's Republic accelerate from ten in 1960 to forty-eight.

So encouraged was it that the policy was striking the right note that Beijing decided to enact a contingency follow-up measure it'd been keeping up its sleeve. To keep the win-win development message at the forefront of the African mind, it decided to raise the level of Chinese exposure across Africa and hence a revamped Xinhua News Agency and an African version of Chinese Central Television were born in Nairobi.

The Xinhua revamping came first, Beijing dispatching a whole new editorial team to the Kenyan capital. Those Beijing considered to have outgrown their usefulness to the African operation were repatriated to China for retraining, replaced by Xi and a phalanx of others already educated as to the importance of the mission and the means of attaining China's desired goals.

It wasn't that those already in situ weren't also aware of the mission and its goals. It was that evidence had come to light that, by venturing outside the Xinhua compound from time to time, some might have become damaged goods.

* * *

After the sprawling grounds that constituted Xinhua's headquarters in central Beijing, the high-walled prison that acted as the agency's compound in Nairobi's Kilimani district left Xi in a state of shock. From its upper stories he could see, hear, taste and smell both the city and the mass of humanity occupying it but could neither touch it nor communicate with either. After his predecessors had begun concocting spurious reasons to set foot outside the compound – showing the clear influence the outside world had had on them on their return – its administrators had been ordered to tighten the screws and ensure the new inmates complied with the regulations to the letter. None was to leave unless all the relevant permissions had been obtained.

What was the point, the cadres in Beijing intoned? The Xinhua staff had everything they needed within the compound. This was where their beds were, their food was, their countrymen were and where their work was. And since their work rarely entailed leaving the compound save to cover visits by Chinese dignitaries, they had no reason to leave. Hence, for their own safety, it was better if they stayed within the walls.

To Xi the miscreant, such close confinement came as little surprise. He'd have been more surprised if he HAD been allowed out. What did surprise him though was that the same rule applied to his colleagues.

Even though all were under strict instruction not to discuss their personal circumstances with one another, it was clear to Xi that most had been seduced into coming and that the means of seduction was duplicity itself.

Somewhat at odds with the protect-you-from-harm explanation for the imprisonment regulation handed down to staff by the Nairobi bureau's administrators, the number one seduction tactic employed by Xinhua's silver-tongued persuaders in Beijing was the rubbishing of the horror stories circulating in China about Africa, Nairobi in particular. Potential recruits were wooed with glowing accounts of Nairobi nightlife, food-to-die-for and a lifestyle to rival anything enjoyed by the rich and famous.

'And there's absolutely no need to worry about the wildlife while on safari,' they cooed. 'It's well known that wild animals have no interest in eating Chinese. Research has proved beyond doubt that, to the animals, the Chinese smell like grass.'

It was only when Xi and his colleagues arrived in Nairobi that they started wondering how on earth their persuaders knew this. All Xinhua staff, the persuaders included, had to follow the same set of rules. None was allowed to roam either the city or the country unaccompanied. In any case, their heavy workloads left them scant opportunity.

Constantly under-staffed, every Xinhua bureau member was doing the work of two, massaging the flood of official government communiqués on Africa into Xinhua-speak and returning them to whence they came for release to an unsuspecting public. Few ever left the compound for the very simple reason that they never had the time and, in any case, their Swahili and English were at best rudimentary.

When they did, it was always as part of an official delegation, locked in a minibus and shepherded to whatever official building the 'story' was taking place in. Then it was back to the compound to write the story up, file the pictures and deal with the mountains of paperwork built up in their absence. Not once in Xi's experience did the news agency's staff ever do what he'd seen western reporters do in the movies – grab their coats and run out of the building on the trail of a scoop or to meet a contact in a dark bar. That just wasn't the way it was done at Xinhua.

And for Xi things hardly changed in ten whole years. Every day for the entire time he'd been a member of the Nairobi bureau staff he'd done virtually the same thing. He got up with all the others in his dormitory, he had breakfast with them, he exercised in the yard with them and went to work with them doing almost exactly what he'd spent the previous ten years doing in Beijing. The only difference was that instead of reconstituting speeches and papers delivered by Chinese bureaucrats in China into Xinhua stories, he was reconstituting speeches and papers delivered by Chinese bureaucrats in Africa into Xinhua stories.

So repetitive was the work that Beijing had to rotate the complement of staff every two or three years to prevent mental disintegration. That was part of the inducement to get people to go. 'Do a couple of years at a foreign bureau,' they were told, 'and a plum job awaits you back in Beijing.'

What they weren't told was that for the entirety of that time they wouldn't be able to communicate with anyone unconnected with the bureau or even see their families.

'Your mission here is to serve the Motherland,' they were told on arrival. 'Your input is vital to the success of China's mission to ensure the image of the People's Republic the world receives is accurate and nothing can be allowed to distract from that goal.'

Fired up with the patriotic zeal instilled in them by their minders, the newcomers threw themselves into the campaign with gusto, enthusiasm which, in Xi's experience, lasted all of six months. After that it gradually began to wane until, after eighteen months or so, all that remained was the shell of enthusiasm and all Xi's workmates could think about was going home.

Without knowing what he knew now, Xi wasn't surprised he was never included in the rotations. His circumstances differed to those of his workmates. They, to a man and woman, had volunteered in return for the promise of that pot of gold on their triumphant return.

So every time the rotation came round without Xi's name on it, he just shrugged. No matter how long it took, he told himself, it was just a matter of time before he got HIS pot of gold, one which would put his workmates' bounty in the shade.

Providing he hadn't been forgotten about altogether, that is. Having been a bystander to some five rotations, it was seeming very much like it.

But then, just when Xi was beginning to worry he'd become the invisible man, in an almost exact replica of his experience at the end of his time at the Xinhua HQ, he got a message. The Nairobi bureau head honcho wanted to see him.

chapter seventeen

'I see from your file that you've been here nearly ten years.'

Oh shit, not this again, thought Xi looking at the woman rarely seen his side of the compound and rumoured to be having a sordid, tawdry affair with one of the agency's African drivers in her private rooms.

'Yes, madam.'

'No need to call me madam. Times have changed since you first joined Xinhua. We're more relaxed about life these days. It's something we're trying to get across to the rest of the world through the style in which Xinhua presents the news, but I expect you've noticed that already.'

'Yes, madam,' said Xi to whom the Xinhua copy still looked as wooden, stilted, one-sided, factually incorrect, misleading, uninformative and self-congratulatory as the day he'd first set eyes on it.

'Ten years. That's a long time. You must feel at home here.'

You tricky bitch, thought Xi. You think my defences are down, don't you? After all this time away from China you think I might have forgotten the traps you people set to get people like me to trip themselves up. You think you can catch me out and get me to condemn myself, by saying yes, meaning I prefer Kenya to China, the place a truly rehabilitated person would rank higher than anywhere else.

Well, you conniving cow, I might have been away a long time but that doesn't mean I'm any less difficult to deal with. You think you're so fucking clever, don't you? Telling me China has changed, that things are now more relaxed. If that's not a shabby little ploy to sucker me into revealing my true feelings for China only to have them noted down and used to extend my sentence to infinity, then China really has changed.

'I was asked,' Xi said with a barely perceptible emphasis on the word 'asked', eyes fixed on a point above the chief administrator's head, 'to come to Africa to serve the Motherland. Until the Motherland has need of me elsewhere, this is where my place is.'

'Most noble,' said the administrator, her eyes scrutinising Xi's face for signs of duplicity. 'Such devotion to duty is commendable. But I'd be surprised if you don't sometimes dwell on things you miss about China. We all do. Your family, for instance...'

At the first mention he'd heard from any of his supervisors about his family in twenty-eight years, Xi struggled to hold his face blank. That one was below the belt. None of his previous supervisors had sunk so low as to remind him of the family he'd been deprived of seeing or communicating with since he was picked up in Tiananmen Square.

Back in the family home in Tianjin, his mother, father, uncles and aunts would all be looking for him, of that he was certain. None would ever have stopped looking, ever have given up petitioning the authorities for news of him since his regular phone calls home from one of Beijing's top universities had suddenly dried up.

In response they might have had some sort of official acknowledgement that his name was on the list of missing persons but that would probably be that. When you were accused of betraying the Motherland, you effectively became a non-person, missing or otherwise. The unedited Xinhua copy that crossed Xi's desk from time to time as much as confirmed it.

Xi had long since stopped fuming about it. These days he used the pain in the way he'd heard people in solitary confinement stuck pins in themselves to keep their feelings alive. Once the feelings and the memories dulled, that was that. You might as well be just another brick in the system's wall. It was what the system wanted.

But as brick-like as he appeared to others, the memory of his treatment and, worse, that of his parents, not only kept him alive but most definitely kicking. One day, he had to keep reminding himself. One day...

Hoping the administrator hadn't noticed his slight pause to compose himself, Xi responded with the answer he'd been rehearsing for moments like this.

'The Motherland is my mother and father,' he said robotically.

'Hmmm,' said his inquisitor, making a note in the file before her.

'Well,' she continued, 'it would seem that your devotion to the Motherland has not been overlooked. I've just received a communiqué from Beijing requesting your services on a special assignment. One that, should you accept it, might keep you occupied beyond the confines of this bureau for some time. Would you consider taking on such an assignment?'

Although the wording was different, it wasn't a million miles from the foreign posting 'request' he'd had from his editor in Beijing all those years ago. Now, as then, Xi knew it to be a test of his rehabilitation. If he'd truly rehabilitated himself it wouldn't be a matter of acceptance. Trusting that the Motherland knew best when it came to his welfare, he'd just do whatever was required of him, no questions asked. Questions meant the exact opposite. Which was why Xi didn't ask the question the administrator was expecting him to ask.

'My role is to serve the Motherland,' said Xi without meeting the administrator's eyes.

'Yes. I think we've established that. But don't you want to know what the assignment is?'

'My role is...'

'Yes, yes. Stop it. You've made your point. Well, it would seem that the Motherland has need of your special skills. It would seem that you originally trained as a geologist, is that correct?'

Xi's blank face almost cracked on hearing a word he hadn't heard since his days labouring in the coalfields. Had he heard that right? Involuntarily, he moved his eyes into line with the administrator's to see if they betrayed any devious double dealing. With none obviously apparent, he felt safe to speak up.

'Yes, madam.'

'Stop calling me madam. Anyway, it seems that that training is what they need to accomplish something that might take some time. They want you to go looking for a mineral I confess I've never heard of. Have you heard of red mercury?'

* * *

To those not familiar with the Xinhua operation, thought Xi, such a request might seem a tad beyond the remit of a news agency's function. Not so when you knew what Xinhua's real role was. It wasn't for nothing that the agency was situated within chopstick chucking distance of the Chinese embassy. As well as being the embassy's mouthpiece, it was its eyes and ears. When not converting the official outpourings of the Chinese Communist Party into Xinhua-ese, the Xinhua staff were charged with monitoring the local media for anything it felt Beijing needed to know.

That didn't mean following anything up or checking the accuracy of the media's stories. Just onpassing what they saw, heard and read to the embassy or direct to Beijing, especially if what they monitored had a Chinese connection – a system that everyone at Xinhua knew to be in some need of revision. When the local media reported in Swahili or English and the Xinhua staff's grasp of either left something to be desired, misunderstandings were, to be charitable, not unknown.

Even so, Beijing persevered. It saw no reason to change a system that once in a while threw up something to make its ears prick up and request further details, requests that inevitably resulted in panic stations at both the embassy and Xinhua. Asked to expand on information filed, both were forced to confront their primary demon – their complete lack of knowledge of the real world going on outside their windows brought about by their complete insulation from it behind impenetrable compound gates.

No one took a job at Xinhua or the embassy expecting to have to deal with real local issues or real local people. All they wanted was to get through their two or three year stints with as little fuss or contact with the outside world as possible living their cosseted insular lives in the little China they'd created within the compound walls. So whenever such a request came in, the compound became a flurry of screeching headless Chinese chickens skittering hysterically hither and thither in search of something to keep Beijing happy and/or someone to pass the buck to.

Xi had noticed just this level of activity the day before he received his summons to the chief administrator's office but hadn't dwelt on it. Nothing he'd seen on the wires seemed to merit all the scurrying around. So far as he knew it'd just been a regular news agency day.

So the hunt for red mercury 'request' had come as something of a shock. He'd heard of it, of course. Who, apart from the chief administrator, hadn't? Even living within a compound effectively sealed off from the real Africa it was difficult to remain completely ignorant of certain African fables of which red mercury was one of the most fabulous.

Being so rare it had achieved mythological status, stories featuring it tended to find themselves being told and re-told in various ways in the local media whenever it was a slow news day or a distraction was needed to prevent something embarrassing to the government getting the front page treatment – thus, in Xi's eyes, making it the Kenyan equivalent of the panda procreation story appearing with embarrassing regularity in the Chinese press.

Pandas and red mercury had something else in common too, Xi mused. He knew precious little about either. Yes, it was mercury and yes, it was reputed to be red. But what form it came in and from what rock type or formation was about as uncertain as its very existence. No author of any red mercury article he'd ever read had claimed to have actually seen it leaving the author no choice but to focus almost entirely on its immeasurable intrinsic value. Red mercury, it was said, was of immense importance in the enhancement of nuclear weapons.

* * *

Standing rigid before the Xinhua administrator as she waited for his response, Xi's mind gyrated. While the underlying reason for her command to see him was self-explanatory, it threw up a whole gamut of peripheral issues, not least the one that interested Xi most. Was this her way of informing him that his time of servitude was at an end?

From being just another miscreant cog in the machine, he was now being charged with the responsibility of locating something that would transform China from second rate nuclear power into one the world's superpowers wouldn't dare mess with. If he wasn't now deemed fully rehabilitated, surely, he thought, his name would not be in the frame for the job. Beijing would be sending in its own team of mineralogists.

In fact, Xi thought, why weren't they? He hadn't done any geological work for nearly thirty years. So why him? Why was a government with trillions of dollars in foreign currency reserves at its disposal asking for a convicted felon's assistance in the search for something that'd make China the envy of the nuclear world. It didn't add up.

Or it didn't until Xi did the sums again. Of course, when you stepped away and looked at it from the government's point of view it made perfect sense. The key was in Xi's own deniability. Specialists in their field would be known to the geological community. If they started showing up and poking around, rats would be smelled.

He, on the other hand, was far from known. In fact, it'd be fair to say, he wasn't known at all. Being spirited into Kenya to spend ten long years hidden from view behind the Xinhua compound walls effectively made him a non-person. If he got caught trying to get his hands on something both Kenya and the West were determined should never reach communist China, the Chinese authorities could deny all knowledge of him. If pressed, they could almost rightly and almost honestly tell the authorities that the description fitted a known subversive who'd disappeared off the face of the earth in China many years earlier. With no record of his identity or arrival in the country, it would be something the Kenyan authorities would have trouble disproving.

The more he thought about it, the more Xi almost applauded China's mendacity. But only until he realised that that anonymity was a double-edged sword. In allowing him to leave the compound had Beijing realised that, with a bit of guile, Xi really could disappear off the face of the earth?

Xi's heart almost stopped beating as the thought struck. Once he was out he was out and the Chinese minders he'd inevitably be accompanied by 'to see you come to no harm' would have trouble persuading the Kenyan authorities to help them apprehend him if he went missing. He almost smiled at the thought of them trying to get the police to help them track down someone they couldn't even prove was in the country. He doubted they'd even try. So his minders would be on their own, Africa was a big place and as Chinese faces on it weren't that unusual these days Xi would have a wood with quite a few trees in it to hide in.

The more he considered the administrator's request, the more attractive it started to look. Everything seemed stacked in his favour. He'd not only be out of the prison he'd been in for nearly three decades but he'd be doing the work he loved, would be seeing the country at the government's expense and he was being handed a golden opportunity to abscond. What was not to like?

Just the one thing. It didn't take him long to realise that his anonymity could well become permanent should he actually stumble upon the mythical substance. On reporting the location back to the authorities they'd undoubtedly ensure the information remained strictly for their eyes only... by effectively plucking his from their sockets.

* * *

So what, thought Xi? If he couldn't put them to good use doing what he'd been trained to do, what use were they to him anyway? In any case, he'd almost put money on never finding the object of the quest. It'd be like looking for a unicorn in the millions of wildebeest rampaging across East Africa on their annual mass migration.

And even if he did stumble across some rock or other that vaguely resembled red mercury he could draw on deniability once again as his means of self-preservation. As the only one with geological training on the mission it wouldn't be difficult convincing his minders it wasn't what they were after.

So yes, he'd told the administrator once all the various permutations had clicked into place in his head, he'd be delighted to take on the task... even if it did cost him his life, he added silently.

In a way it'd be setting him free. As a man deprived of reputation, assets, identity and freedom what was the point of living anyway. He was forty-five years old, he'd been unjustly deprived of family, friends, career and liberty for well over half that time and had received no indication when the torture would end. If this was 'life', it was something he wouldn't miss that much. The only thing he would miss was the chance of getting even with his jailers.

'Oh my God!' Xi just managed to prevent himself shouting out loud as the thought struck.

'Fuck me. That's it! I've got you, you bastards.'

The agency, he'd just realised, had handed him the means of retribution on a plate. Why the fuck hadn't he spotted it straight off?

chapter eighteen

Chinese rockhounds scouring the African countryside for minerals were hardly an unheard-of phenomenon by the time Xi received his mission request. With oil and ores making up four-fifths of Africa's China-bound exports, battalions of Chinese exploration specialists were everywhere, flying into the continent over container-crammed ships ferrying the product of the geologists' quest in the opposite direction.

The visual image of this cyclical swap amused Xi. 'You get people and the odd wad of notes paid into an account of your choice and we get everything that can be dug up and shipped,' seemed to be the unspoken undertone to China's African charm offensive.

Just what Africa needs, thought Xi. More people.

In the period he was allowed to prepare for his first exploratory trip Xi's research showed it was mostly the metals China's geologists were after – iron, copper, zinc, titanium and the like along with the more precious metals and rare earths vital in the manufacture of electronic components.

The figures in official reports on Chinese/African trade made Xi's head spin. In the ten years he'd been at Xinhua's Nairobi bureau, annual trade between the two had grown eightfold to over three hundred billion dollars. In another five years it was forecast to reach four hundred and, if all went to plan, by 2020 Chinese direct investment across Africa was expected to double from its current fifty billion dollar total, most of it aimed at keeping the continent's oil and mineral output flowing.

'Well,' thought Xi, 'if they've got that sort of money to throw about I might just ask if we can buy decent Chinese rice for our trip. The grit they bulk this cheap African crap out with is busting my teeth.'

The 'request denied' response Xi got left him smiling. By being so miserly, all his masters had done was lend weight to a suspicion growing in Xi's mind that all was not as it seemed *a propos* the official version of the China/Africa relationship.

Non-Chinese analyses of China's economy he'd rooted out suggested that funds for his trip around Kenya wasn't the only thing China was being economical with. China's economic growth figures, said the analyses, were 'somewhat overstated'.

If that was true, thought Xi, then if China isn't doing half as well as it says, the effect would be obvious. Places like Africa would begin seeing inward Chinese investment drying up.

With the world still reeling from the effects of the great global banking crash of 2008, Xi had always wondered how it was possible that China had come through it as unscathed as the government claimed. If you believed what Beijing said, you'd think China was above the rest of the world's economy. But since there was most definitely no disconnection – more the opposite – how could it be that while the rest of the world floundered, China was registering growth figures the West would kill for?

The official version, of course, was that under the country's socialism-with-Chinese characteristics system, the wild financial swings seen in the West were all but impossible in China. Being state-controlled, the government crowed, the banks and the country's industry were bombproof.

Xi was no economist but he knew a glossing-over when he heard it, a suspicion that was hardly dented by being denied decent rice. If Xinhua couldn't run to that one basic commodity, maybe, just maybe, things back home weren't as rosy as the stories arriving on his desk for polishing suggested.

Even he could work out that with the crippled West cutting back on Chinese imports, China's earnings would suffer. Without those earnings, it was self-evident that China would be cutting back on industrial production. Which meant it'd need less in the way of raw materials to feed the factories. Less raw materials it got from where? Africa.

The upshot? If China needed less from Africa, less Chinese money would be going into the continent to keep production going. Without that money, Africans would have less in their pockets to spend and that would mean them economising on certain things. Rice, for example.

In Xi's estimation only one outcome was possible from such economising. More grit would be added to bulk the rice out and there were only ever going to be two winners in this vicious, tooth-busting circular game – the grit suppliers and the dentists.

As reasonable as Xi considered his Chinese economic downturn theory to be, he wasn't slow to realise it had one little flaw. If China's economy really was slowing and if it really was true that China needed less in the way of raw materials from Africa, why was he being dispatched to try and locate one that hadn't even been proved to exist? Funding what could be an expensive exploration made no sense… but then again, thought Xi, the same could be said of a lot of what Beijing and Xinhua did. His own attachment to an organisation whose work was about as far removed from his geological specialism as it was possible to get was a prime example.

Even so, Xi tried to be charitable. As detached as his masters seemed to be from reality, in the case of this mission there might just be method in the madness. Non-Chinese articles he'd come across were of the opinion that Beijing was using the mountains of cash amassed from previous years' exports to ramp up its military might as a hedge against relations with the West deteriorating. But as mighty as the Chinese military machine got, Beijing was not blind to the fact that it was still no match for the combined forces of the capitalist world.

Which, thought Xi, is probably where red mercury comes in. If China had the fabled, weaponry-enhancing substance in its possession – or even if it was suspected of having it – the country's detractors would think at least twice before doing anything silly.

That, said the articles Xi had read, was closer to happening than anyone was prepared to admit. The US was already jumping up and down in reaction to China's construction of man-made islands in international waters closer to the Philippines than China and US hawks were urging a ramping up of US presence in the region on the suspicion that the islands were being constructed to accommodate Chinese military bases.

China, naturally, denied the accusation. Territorial expansion, it continued to insist, was not part of Chinese government policy.

'Try telling that to the peoples of South East Asia,' thought Xi. Even Xinhua was reporting a worsening of relations between China and Vietnam over the growing and not infrequently hostile Chinese presence in Vietnamese fishing grounds.

And it wasn't just South East Asia experiencing a flexing of Chinese muscles. Here in Africa, China was making its presence felt in more ways than just economic. The western media was reporting Chinese arms exports to Sudan and parts of southern Africa and China itself had given up denying it intended building a military base in the tiny Horn of Africa enclave of Djibouti. To support the Chinese fleet in its mission to protect the East African shipping lanes from Somali pirates, went the official reasoning to no one's belief or surprise.

The upshot of all this was that China seemed to be making more enemies than friends around the world and, despite all the 'help' it kept trumpeting it was giving Africa and other developing nations, it was even antagonising the people it espoused to be helping.

Amongst the articles Xi unearthed were any number detailing seething African anger over China's bulldozing of local considerations when it came to the making of a quick buck. Cheap Chinese imports were putting African clothing and footwear companies out of business and violent protests were erupting with growing frequency over the way African workers were treated in Chinese-owned operations, the mines in particular.

The articles clearly showed these were far from isolated incidents and that the harmonious sweetness and light relationship China insisted existed between the Chinese and their African hosts had a side that was growing darker by the day.

South Africa's then-president Jacob Zuma summed it up nicely, thought Xi. Unless things changed, he said, China's presence in his country would ultimately become 'unsustainable'.

With such sentiments becoming common currency in all quarters, China, said the commentators, was feeling not a little unloved and insecure. But rather than change the way it operated to restore its detractors' confidence, the more likely outcome was for Beijing to go on the defensive. All the hostility arriving at its door could well result in a circling of the wagons, shutting the West out in much the same way as happened during the darkest days of Maoism.

Despite his collar-and-tie appearance, China's president since 2012, Xi Jinping, was at heart an unreconstructed Maoist, said the commentators, and if pushed too far could easily decide to take the country inward again. Raise his hackles and he could well do what Mao did, only worse. He could decide to isolate China from the rest of the world. But unlike last time it'd be the rest of the world that'd suffer most. The West would not only find itself without the manufacturing hub it'd grown so reliant on but suddenly discover it'd been excluded from a vital export market for its own products.

Worse, push China to the point at which its back was against the wall and this time Beijing wouldn't be afraid to come out fighting.

'Mess with us,' went the bellicose posturing between the lines of Chinese diplomatic nicety, 'and don't be surprised if you have China's military might to deal with.'

And that's without red mercury, thought Xi. If China gets its hands on that, the real surprise would be anyone being stupid enough to try.

* * *

Good Chinese rice, Xi discovered during the expeditions' planning stage, wasn't the only thing he was being denied. Neither was he being allowed money for accommodation, a fund for prising red mercury location information out of the locals or his own vehicle.

'In the interests of utilising Xinhua's resources to maximum effect,' said the chief administrator, 'it has been decided that an outside contractor will be engaged to provide both transport and tented accommodation thus allowing you to concentrate fully on the task in hand. Your responsibility will rest entirely on selecting the locations worthy of investigation and communicating said locations to the contractor via the assisting team that is to accompany you on what the contractor will be told is a mission to track down and film a very rare bird, the nechisar nightjar.

'All communications with the contractor are to be conducted via your assisting team. At no point are you to interface with the contractor directly. Is that understood?'

Perfectly, thought Xi. I know exactly what you're telling me – that you still don't trust me. You think I'm going to blab about the mission's real purpose to either the contractor or others we meet along the way. Hence not being allowed to use hotels. You think I'll get drunk in the bar and let slip that we're really on the trail of something that will make China the envy of the military world.

'It tells me something else too,' said Xi to himself. 'It tells me that reports of a China changed out of all recognition from the China that lost touch with reality in Mao's time are grossly overstated.'

While he could understand the edict banning him from talking to the tour guide directly, the ban on hotel use and the decision to employ a tour guide in the first place was sheer lunacy. If ever there was a way of drawing attention to the expedition it was a bunch of Chinese setting up camp within sight of an hotel whose bar would inevitably be used by the one member of their party who wouldn't have to answer to Beijing should details of the mission leak out.

'This is madness,' Xi muttered inwardly, 'but who am I to question the judgement of those in authority? As nothing more than a humble servant of the state, it's not my role to call into question the decisions made by higher powers even though they do look designed to make the mission blow up in their faces.'

As the thought struck, prompting Xi to smile internally, he instantly regretted it. The administrator's next words gave him the distinct impression that either his face must have betrayed his thoughts or she was able to read them.

'And in case you're wondering,' she went on, 'the decision to hire an outsider to provide transport was not taken without a great deal of consideration as to the cost and security risks involved.

'To begin with, both our own drivers are city-born and won't know the outlying areas as well as a professional safari operator' – and anyway you're shagging one of them and don't fancy a lengthy period of celibacy, added Xi under his breath.

'Secondly, we can't spare the four wheel drive. We might need it for Xinhua operations.

'Third, it has been decided that using an outside contractor will actually add to the security of the operation. No one will look twice at a professional safari vehicle ferrying a group of Chinese around the country. They'll just be regarded as ordinary tourists. A Xinhua vehicle will attract far more attention.

'Fourth, it's not going to cost as much as might be thought. There's a small scale operation one of the drivers knows which charges far less than the Abercrombie & Kents of the safari world. Taking into account that this outfit will not only provide the vehicle, specialist knowledge of the countryside and all the necessary camping equipment, the cost of hiring it compares well with having to purchase all the equipment needed to mount an exclusively Xinhua-run expedition.'

And fifth, thought Xi without being able to stop himself, you can bet your boots your driver toyboy is doing OK out of it too.

Sealed off from Africa for the entirety of his ten years with Xinhua's Nairobi bureau he might have been, but Xi had still managed to grasp some inkling of the way the African mind worked. Not least that, in Africa, the something-for-nothing principle did not apply. When there was a chance of skimming something off the top, it was simply standard African practise not to let that chance go begging. In which case, pledged Xi silently, if the price given to the administrator by the driver bore any relation to the price given to the driver by the safari operator he'd eat anything that gave even a passing resemblance to red mercury.

He was pretty confident of one other thing too. With the Xinhua drivers unlikely to know anyone at the top end of the safari business, the operations of the ones they were likely to know would almost undoubtedly be shabby, two-bit, one man-and-his-hyena affairs using vehicles that would look more at home in a museum.

In the event, Xi wasn't far wrong but that was the last thing occupying his mind as he prepared his end of the mission. Far more important was making it look like he was going after the fabled substance while ensuring the search, and thus his tour across a country he'd been in for ten years and never allowed to see, lasted for as long as decently possible.

The key would be in the geological maps of the region he'd persuaded the administrator to acquire for him. Maps only he could interpret and which were central to his plan of convincing all involved that, for maximum likelihood of success, they should start at the top and work their way south.

Actually, that wasn't a bad plan, thought Xi. They could get the north Kenya badlands bit out of the way first then concentrate on the more scenic tourist hotspots in the east, south, central and west.

Whether the plan was approved or not didn't really matter. The only thing Xi had to make sure of was that none of his party stumbled on anything that even faintly resembled red mercury. If they did, it'd put the rest of his carefully worked-out sightseeing jaunt in serious jeopardy.

chapter nineteen

Moses wasn't generally the worrying kind. But the liquid nitrogen in the woman's voice and the stones she had for eyes left him quaking in his flip-flops. Her message had been received loud and clear. It wasn't just his job he'd lose if word got out that the request had come from her. It would be any hope he had of adding to the array of progeny he'd already produced. Without the equipment to produce any more, the tone in her voice had told him, she could well be the last 'encounter' he ever had.

So no, he went to great lengths to assure Xinhua's chief administrator, he wouldn't be blabbing that he'd just been asked to find a safari guide for his Chinese boss.

'As the life and soul of the integrity,' he'd warbled, 'even me, madame, I will go to hell and high water to stay as silent as the driven snow.'

Slinking furtively off into the night from her private rooms, just one thing played on his mind. He hoped to hell she'd got the message. It wasn't easy to tell when the woman he'd just rent asunder with his very un-Oriental manhood was still sweating with orgasmic paroxysm and whose grasp of English was even worse than his.

The concern stayed with him all the way to the bar he went to recover from his regular after-hours visits to a woman whose rapacious capacity for sexual gymnastics made his own hyperactive libido look decidedly limp.

Sitting over his usual White Cap, this time he ordered up a

chang'aa chaser in the hope that Kenya's version of instant death would inspire the answer to another tricky problem – how to get Kearney to take the job without telling him who he'd be working for.

His Irish friend's tight – a more appropriate word for it Moses couldn't imagine – operation was perfect for what she wanted… a small time safari operator who'd do precisely what he was told and query nothing except the price. If he hadn't known she didn't know him, Moses could have sworn she'd been talking about the man he'd first come across in one of Nairobi's dodgiest car part stores haggling with the dealer over the already giveaway price of a Landrover tie rod end.

Moses was drawn to the man from the moment he slammed his business card down on the counter and, in quite passable street Swahili, told the dealer not only what he thought of him but unless he was prepared to be reasonable he'd better start getting his affairs in order.

It was the logo on the card that won Moses and the rest of the store's customers over. Made up from the initials of his company name, the Kearney's Kenya logo reduced everyone who saw it to knee-slapping mirth.

KK, the universally-used abbreviation for the 'something small' *kitu kidogo* illegal inducement euphemism, Moses was to later discover, fitted Kearney's operation perfectly. Constantly broke, the man would not only do anything for a buck but wasn't that fussy about who he did it with or for.

So when it came to thinking of someone to undertake the Chinese safari, Moses' thoughts started and stopped with Kearney. Not only did he fit the bill to perfection but he was a *mzungu* thereby making him far easier to fleece for a commission than any of the Kenyan safari guides Moses knew. To a man they'd tell him to roundly go fuck himself and Moses wasn't in the business of letting such a KK opportunity – from both ends of the spectrum – go to waste.

It was the first thing Moses had secured from the woman who'd struggled to convey her requirements to him in English.

'Want safari man take Chinese film doing,' she'd told him. 'Ver special filming. You find man, and for sure get *kay-kay*.'

'But no talking about,' she'd commanded, fixing him with her stone eyes. 'Talk talk and live rest of life in interesting times,' she'd said, drawing one finger across her throat while pointing to the ever-present bulge in his recently-donned trousers with another.

It took Moses less than a day to accomplish his mission. The one thing he knew for certain about Kearney was that unless he was out on safari, a rare occurrence these days, he'd be propping up a bar in one of three favoured watering holes.

In the end Moses found him in the place he hoped he'd be. Psy's was Kearney's last resort, the place he went when his credit at the Norfolk and the Carnivore had run out. Being at Psy's meant the man was on his uppers and therefore less likely to be selective about the sort of jobs that came his way.

Even so, it had taken two beers to bring the Irishman round. Kearney was a tough cookie, thought Moses on his way out. He did that on purpose, umming and ahhing and not showing his hand until he had a second bottle in it. The bastard.

Nevertheless he had his man and the promise of some KK and all without identifying who it was he'd actually be working for. So far as Kearney was concerned, his tour group was just a Chinese film crew in need of a specialist guide to help them find and film some rare species they'd reveal to him when the time came. Did he want the job? A clink of bottles later and the deal was done.

* * *

As reluctant as he was about giving an opinion on anything lest it get noted down and used against him, Xi knew he could avoid the moment no longer. He'd been asked what his plan of action was and now he had no option but to run it past those with the power to make or break him.

Moving hesitantly towards the map of Kenya pinned to the wall of the administrator's office, Xi looked guardedly at the administrator and the two security men she'd selected to be his constant companions on the expedition.

Three blank, inscrutable faces looked back giving nothing away.

'As requested,' he tried to say, finding nothing coming out other than a high-pitched squeak.

'A-hem,' he tried again. 'As per the request of our comrade administrator, I have been studying the geological maps of the region with the intention of pinpointing the areas offering the greatest potential for locating the substance sought and, after much consideration, have reached the following conclusion.

'If the substance is to be found anywhere, it is most likely to be in areas that have been subjected to the greatest tectonic disturbance. It is for that reason that it would seem appropriate that the first phase of the search is concentrated on this area,' he said, pointing to the central Great Rift Valley belt stretching from the border with Ethiopia down to Lake Victoria.

'In order to narrow the search down, I then conducted a close examination of the literature relating to the petrology of the region. Although not an expert on this aspect of geological specialisation, it would seem from the literature that the greatest potential lies in the northern Rift,' he said, raising his finger to circle an area encompassing the north Kenya badlands and the southernmost provinces of Ethiopia.

'However, since no investigation of the Ethiopian sector has been authorised, that restricts the initial search area to northern

Kenya and, with your permission madam administrator, I would propose that we start here,' he said, tapping Lake Turkana on the map.

'From photographs I've seen of the area, it would appear that the rugged geomorphology of the region is consistent with it having been subjected to massive horst block disturbance and that this disturbance has given rise to sufficient outcrops to facilitate a reasonable assessment of the transformatory nature of the Pliocene zonal stratigraphy and thus of the primary metamorphosis.

'It for that reason that I would recommend the initial survey focus on this and the interstitial zone between the Gombe basalts and the quartzo-feldspathic grit assemblage formed between the Cretaceous and Pleistocene.'

Scanning the faces for a reaction to his proposal, Xi was relieved to see only blankness looking back. His tactic of infusing his presentation with a bewildering array of geological terminology to befuddle his audience and thus gain the upper hand in the planning process seemed to be working. Or it had until the administrator spoke up.

'What's petrol got to do with it?' she scowled. 'That's not what we're after.'

The comment first stunned Xi then, after a moment's pause to work out what she was talking about, encouraged him. By revealing she had no idea that petrology was the term given to the study of the origin, content and make-up of rocks, the administrator had effectively told him he could tell them virtually anything he wanted without fear of contradiction.

It was a power he exercised to the full in the week between his geological *tour de force* and the planned expedition start-date.

'Having studied the region in detail,' he told them at the subsequent travel planning meeting, 'might I suggest taking this route to Lake Turkana?' he said, pointing to the lesser travelled

159

tracks that would take them east of the most direct route and through Samburu territory.

'While it might take a little longer, it passes through other potentially red mercury-bearing strata which, in any case, will need to be assessed should the Turkana investigation prove fruitless.'

When the three other members of the planning committee reluctantly murmured their agreement, Xi metaphorically punched the air. He'd always wanted to make contact with the Samburu, a tribe he'd read were known as the Butterfly People after their love of nature and their gentle easygoing attitude to life. After ten years looking at the same set of walls, he reasoned, a bit of a diversion off the beaten track to enjoy himself in an area renowned for its spectacular scenery was no more than he deserved.

And anyway, he told himself, he wasn't really lying. The route really would take them through other possible, but highly unlikely, red mercury-bearing areas where he could indulge in his real passion – fossil-hunting.

* * *

Xi wasn't the only one who'd been busy that week. While he was poring over maps under the compound's sole, solitary tree, the security goons were shadowing Moses on every shopping mission he was sent on by the administrator. Having provided him with a substantial quantity of cash to purchase the necessary items for the team's safari, the administrator's anxiety levels entered alopecia territory every time he ventured out with the agency's money.

Together with the funds she'd provided to pay the safari deposit Kearney had demanded, he had enough to stage a rapid disappearing act across the Tanzanian border to devote the rest of his life to satisfying the needs of every unfulfilled female between Dar es Salaam and Dodoma.

If such an intention had been on Moses' mind, the security guards' presence was sufficient deterrent to convince him to put them on hold until a better opportunity arose. For the moment, he decided, he'd just devote his energies to shopping and, by the time he was done, Moses had everything the administrator deemed necessary for the expedition – up to and including the crisp new safari jackets, shorts and hats the three-man team sported as they left the compound to meet up with the man charged with getting them to their target destination.

It wasn't just Xi who groaned inwardly on being told it was what they needed to wear if they were to pass for Chinese tourists. Neither he nor either of the security men had ever seen a professional wildlife film crew decked out in such attire. Their very profession precluded such a laughable eventuality.

Even so, none spoke up to question the administrator's instruction. While the goons' brainwashing ensured they'd accept without comment any directive handed down by a superior, Xi's determination to avoid rocking the boat until the time was right was at peak amplitude.

'Just one more step,' he told himself as the compound gates swung open, 'and I can say goodbye to this prison forever... and then to these bloody stupid costumes.'

chapter twenty

Xi could hardly contain himself on finally getting beyond the Xinhua confines. But doing it before daybreak so the agency minibus could deliver them to the Hurlingham shopping centre half an hour before Kearney was due pick them up? That, he thought, was taking caution a bit far.

OK, he understood there was a need for secrecy on this mission. But since, so far as their guide knew, they were just a group of Chinese film makers, wouldn't it seem a bit odd meeting them in a shopping centre car park rather than at one of the big hotels?

Oh yeah. Right. They were banned from using hotels. Which just went to show how paranoid Xinhua and the embassy were and, probably, how broke China really was.

It was a suspicion that the state of the vehicle Xinhua had hired for the expedition did little to dispel. Even the security men's faces nearly cracked on seeing it pull into the centre's car park.

Here was a vehicle that had undoubtedly seen serious action, mostly in war zones by the look of it. If there was a panel on it which didn't look like it'd been repaired by a gorilla with a sledge-hammer none of them could spot it.

The driver looked like he'd received similar treatment. Big and brawny with hair spouting wildly from every exposed body part, next to his passengers in their brand new safari outfits the man not only looked like a beggar with a wardrobe problem but gave every impression of being rather too closely related to the gorilla for comfort.

As he roared into the car park, slewing to a halt in a cloud of dust, the three expedition members eyed one another warily. Without having to say so, all were having the same, simultaneous thought. If this was the administrator's idea of remaining inconspicuous, perhaps she should get out more.

'Hello there,' the gorilla's cousin grinned at them holding out a gnarled paw. 'Grand day for it, eh? Kearney's the name and this here's the infamous Millennium Falcon – fastest craft in the universe to anyone who's seen Star Wars. Well, maybe there's one or two which could give her a run for her money these days but back when she was built… no contest. None at all.

'So it's off to Turkana is it,' he said, tentatively withdrawing a hand that remained un-shook. 'Grand place for filming. Hot though. Hope you've got something a bit cooler than those safari outfits packed away. Gonna need them. OK, let's get loaded.'

'What did he say?' Xi asked the more senior of his security goon travelling companions.

'Something about wars and the need to get loaded.'

'Fuck. No one said anything about bringing a gun. Have you got one?'

The security man's blank look by way of return told Xi everything he needed to know.

*　*　*

Despite its looks, the Millennium Falcon's interior was surprisingly comfy, thought Xi. The fabric seats, while scuffed and stained, were especially welcome. Xi could imagine how hot the black plastic coverings of the Xinhua minibus seats would get if left in the sun too long. Which was probably why those of his Xinhua colleagues who were allowed out always wore long trousers. Peeling bare Chinese legs off melting plastic wouldn't be a lesson needing to be learned twice.

In fact the whole of the car's interior seemed in good order for the vehicle's obvious age and as they bumped their way north between the potholes making up the bulk of the A2 Thika Road, Xi hoped the engine was equally well cared for. As much as he was enjoying being out of the compound at last, he didn't much fancy breaking down in *shifta* country, a place reputed to be full of brigands who shot first and asked questions never.

But that wasn't just yet. First would come a relatively secure ride up to and around the eastern flank of Mount Kenya, a mountain high enough to have a glacier at its peak. It was a sight Xi anticipated seeing like a small boy. Imagine, he kept telling himself excitedly, snow and ice at the equator. What it must be like to actually climb it! Maybe one day, when this is all over…

Xi's excitement increased with every milepost passed, every town ticked off. Thika, tick. Murang'a, tick. Kirinyanga, tick. Each one a step closer to seeing the mountain and each one encountered and discarded like a layer of wrapping paper in a game of pass the parcel. Soon, very soon, the last layer would be torn off and there it would be. Unless, of course, it was cloudy.

Xi almost squealed with delight when Kearney rounded a bend and pointed to the left. The snowy peak, just visible above some low cloud, was silhouetted by the sun sinking slowly down behind it.

To Xi it matched anything he'd ever seen in China but just in time restrained himself from saying so. The expressionless faces of his travelling companions told him that such displays of wonder and enchantment were reserved for China only. Everywhere else was to receive nothing but a 'not as good as China' face and that any departure from the official line was tantamount to spitting on the Chinese flag.

As Xi struggled to contain himself, a thought occurred. So why, if nothing compares to China, are so many Chinese travelling abroad these days? A million and a half each year to Africa, he'd read, and upwards of fifty thousand to Kenya alone. If they're not especially impressed with the wildlife and the scenery, then that means what the western media was saying about Africa's Chinese visitors must be true. Most, apart from the thousands coming voluntarily – or, like him, involuntarily – to work, must be masquerading as tourists. Tourists whose real intention was to flood the markets with cheap Chinese goods, put African textile manufacturers out of business and smuggle illicit ivory back to China. There was no other explanation for it.

Except, of course, that there was. Openly flouting the official line, they came to marvel at the very thing he was currently marvelling at. The only difference was that they paid tens of thousands of yuan for the privilege. And here was he, a prisoner of the state, getting the treatment for nothing.

The irony of it all left him unable to stifle the grin he'd been wanting to grin for the last twenty-eight years. A grin he noticed that was being returned in spades by the driver via his rear view mirror.

That grin and the almost imperceptible wink he delivered left Xi certain of two things. Not only was the driver rather more perceptive than he looked but that he and Kearney were going to get along like the pair of favourite chopsticks tucked away in the pocket of Xi's stiff new safari jacket.

chapter twenty-one

Smitten by the glimpse of the summit's peak the evening before, Xi was up before daybreak in the hope of witnessing it being lit up by the first rays of the sun. Slipping silently from the tent he shared with his minders at the camping spot Kearney had chosen, Xi skirted the still snoring driver in the hammock he'd slung between the Landrover and a tree and waited.

It was a sight he knew would stay with him for the rest of his life. Even at a distance and without the aid of binoculars Xi could see the glacier at the top gradually light up pale yellow, then turn pink, then finally reveal its true, startlingly white majesty before the whole mountain disappeared beneath a tide of cloud piling up from its base.

Xi remained spellbound for several minutes hoping desperately to see it reappear. Only when sure it had gone for good did he tear his eyes away to focus on the other thing occupying his mind. While setting up camp the previous evening Xi had noticed an interesting rocky outcrop nearby and wanted to take a closer look before the driver woke up. Witnessing one of his party hacking away at the scenery they'd ostensibly come to film might lead to questions that could signal an abrupt end to Xi's sightseeing tour. His minders didn't like questions.

By the time Xi crept back to camp to blow life into the near-dead fire and get the kettle on, he'd both found and not found what he'd been looking for. While no trace of the mercury-bearing mineral cinnabar could be seen, there was, not surprisingly, abundant evidence of the transformation of the original strata into metamorphic rock.

Xi knew from the geological maps they were already straddling the Great Rift Valley's tectonic shift and it'd have been more surprising if he hadn't found evidence of the original rock being subjected to immense heat and pressure during the upheaval. That heat had been enough to melt it and produce mineral-bearing veins as it cooled, a process not unlike his own transformation, Xi mused. It wasn't just the rock that'd been bent and pounded and reshaped into a whole new being streaked with veins of fire.

Staring into the campfire's gradually re-igniting embers, Xi realised these too reflected his own condition. But unlike the fire, he knew he'd need to smoulder a while longer before bursting into life. Now was not the time, and anyway his minders were already crawling from their tent and the driver was looking at him with one bleary eye telling him in no uncertain terms that he was treading on thin ice. It wasn't the client's job to make the coffee.

* * *

It took two more days of driving to get to Lake Turkana, not because it was far away or because the vehicle wasn't, as claimed, the fastest thing in the universe, but because Xi wanted it that way.

Determined not to waste the opportunity of spending as much time as possible in a region rich with geological wonder, Xi had asked his 'assistants' to communicate to the driver his preference to dawdle. Officially, it was so Xi could hop out whenever he felt the need to rush off into the bush to examine tracks that could be those of the bird they'd now told the driver they'd come to film. Unofficially, it was so Xi could disappear behind rocky outcrops to do more hacking and, hopefully, get a glimpse of the local inhabitants, the stone age Samburu.

Only once did Xi get his wish and then only at a distance. Stopping near a creek for lunch, as the whole party went to cool off in the clear trickling stream a group of children clad only in animal skins appeared on top of the hillock separating the party from the Falcon. Shrieking with laughter in response to Kearney's wave, the children grinned great toothy grins at one another then ran off leaving the party to their soak and Xi to examine the handful of glittering flakes he'd just scooped from the river bed.

The driver's eyes popped on spotting what was in Xi's hand.

'Is it? Could it be?' they said.

'Nah,' said Xi's in response. 'Just iron pyrites. Fool's gold. And a bit of mica. No great cause for celebration unless, like me, you're looking for evidence of more intense metamorphic activity.' The flakes told Xi they were definitely closing in on something of interest. But what, precisely, remained uncertain. He'd know it when he saw it.

He'd also know the thief when he saw him. He'd be wearing the smelly, sweaty trainers Xi had left hanging on the Falcon's wing mirror to air while they bathed.

This was something he hadn't been warned about. Light-fingeredness wasn't something that featured strongly in the literature he'd read about the Samburu. The books were far more interested in telling the reader how good-natured and fun-loving the tribe was compared to their close relations, the lofty Maasai.

Neither did the books dwell on the tetchiness of the Turkana people. That, the party was to discover on finally reaching their destination, was something else they'd have been interested in knowing about in advance. It was a tetchiness that had led to them having to break one of the cardinal rules of the expedition and book themselves into a local hotel for a couple of nights.

Knowing they'd have to report the departure from regulations to the administrator, all three were left wondering how to put it to her that they'd had no choice. How, they wondered, were they to tell her they'd effectively been banned from camping on the Turkana tribe's territory after the driver had declined the offer of having sex with the chief's daughters. It was an explanation they somehow doubted the administrator would fully accept or understand and had already started bracing themselves for the repercussions.

Two nights in the Lodwar Hotel and a further four under canvas in a spot the driver knew was far enough away from the Turkana chief's village to avoid antagonising him further was enough to tell Xi he'd seen as much as he needed.

While there was much evidence of metamorphic activity in the rocks around the lake, he'd failed to find anything resembling red mercury but had unearthed any number of interesting fossils that would go straight into his own collection.

What's more, being left largely alone to get on with his rock work as the other members of the 'film' team pretended to get scene-setting footage for the film they were pretending to make, he'd had the time to work out how to fulfil his own real purpose of the trip.

Now he knew the habits of his co-travellers, he knew precisely how his plan for getting even with China was going to be accomplished. In return for condemning him iniquitously to a life of incarceration and celibacy, China would shortly be discovering that its secret was a secret no longer. It would be discovering that the rest of the world had been alerted to a snippet of news equally as tantalising as evidence of the existence of a bird known only from the remains of a few tattered wing parts.

It was an apt parallel, thought Xi. The nechisar nightjar was every bit the equal of red mercury when it came to mythological legends of the African bush.

* * *

Ever since being acquainted with his mission to find it, Xi had been wondering how to get news of the hunt for red mercury to the rest of the world. At first he could see no way of achieving that end. But then the Xinhua administrator had unwittingly solved the problem for him. By deciding to hire in an outside contractor, all but one of the links in the chain was in place. The only thing missing was the means of alerting a non-Chinese to what the team was really up to.

After a week in the bush, it came to him. Now he knew more of the rest of the team's evening habits, it was just a matter of waiting for the right combination of factors to align themselves.

Timing, thought Xi, was everything. Let the cat out of the bag too soon and he risked word of his secret communication with the outside world leaking back to his minders. Too late, and he'd never get another chance should the plan backfire.

In the end, Xi plumped for the final stop on their tour, the campsite at Lake Baringo.

Having found nothing of interest on the eastern flank of the Great Rift Valley or around Lake Turkana, Xi had ordered the driver to head south down the central section to an area containing two other lakes, Bogoria and Baringo.

It was Bogoria that interested the ever-professional Xi the most. Its scalding hot springs were where, if anywhere, the source of mercury would be found. Being a sulphide formed when highly-pressurised, volcanically-heated water rose to the surface and lost its pressure, this was where the mercury-bearing mineral cinnabar was most likely to occur. It wasn't that lakes Turkana and Baringo didn't also have hot springs, it was that Bogoria's were the hottest, spurting violently out of the ground and turning the surrounding mud a deep, crimson red.

Most of the redness was a heat-loving algae. Xi knew that. But there was a chance some wasn't. Some could be the product of minute crystals of cinnabar collecting in the mud, crystals so red they were used to make the brilliant scarlet paint vermilion.

To Xi's mind, this is probably where the fable of red mercury originated. You'd expect silver mercury to come from a source rock of the same colour. So when globules of ordinary mercury were found oozing from a red mineral, the myth of red mercury had not only been born but perpetuated by those with an interest in seeing it didn't die thereby leaving the fabled substance the stuff of legend.

Xi's plan was to ensure that a myth wasn't the only thing being perpetuated. News that the Chinese were on the hunt for red mercury would gain momentum with each person the news reached – starting with the water delivery boy at Lake Baringo.

As night fell and the expedition members prepared to turn in for the night, Xi called the boy over and while the goons were intent on their usual evening card game and the safari operator had disappeared into the bushes to answer the call of nature, showed him the phial of ordinary mercury he'd brought with him.

'You see?' asked Xi in broken English and Swahili sweeping his hand out and around in the internationally-known 'somewhere?' gesture. 'We look same same but red.'

Prompting nothing but a blank look from the boy Xi tried again, this time pulling out a pen and paper, scribbling down a phone number and handing it to the boy with a few shilling notes.

'You see red mercury, you call. *Mingi shillingi, sawa sawa*?' said Xi in a voice raised loud enough to ensure the boy got the message.

'Good,' thought Xi, smiling happily to himself as the boy scampered away. 'It's done. That'll teach the bastards to ruin my life.'

* * *

Ruin was also what Kearney was contemplating as he and Ryan headed for the Bushwacker Camp bar a week later. Not only had he lost a lucrative contract thanks to his failure to shag a Turkana chief's daughter compounded, indisputably, by an intervention from that bastard Mwangi, but now he was having to use up precious resources on a new tie rod end.

The day after arriving back in Nairobi to resupply for the next stage of the Chinese safari, Moses had tracked him down to tell him he needn't bother. The 'film' team had changed their minds after being made to stay at a hotel when they'd specifically ordered a camping-only safari. So they'd be making alternative arrangements from now on and Kearney could sing for the rest of the money they owed him.

Having only Moses as a contact source with his clients – the Chinese ordering Kearney to drop them at the same place he'd picked them up – all Kearney could do was flap his jaw. Without knowing where they stayed, there was no way of putting the screws on his 'clients' to recoup either the outstanding amount or that part of the deposit he'd had to part with to cover their hotel bill. In short, he'd been Great Walled, he thought, just like half the Africans who'd ever done business with the Chinese cheetah.

If Kearney thought Moses could be 'encouraged' into helping him find them, the droplets of sweat that appeared on the man's forehead when he suggested it told him otherwise. Moses was clearly more scared of them than he was of Kearney.

So once again, Kearney found himself back at square one, potless and without hope of ever being anything other.

Or maybe not. The safari, he reflected, hadn't been a complete waste of time. It had thrown up something Kearney knew to be of value. But how to convert it to hard cash he knew not.

One broken tie rod on his way to Mombasa, an evening in the Bushwacker bar with Ryan after rescuing the Falcon from a roadside ditch and a jolting ride on Kenya Railways later, he had it. It wasn't without risk, Kearney was well aware of that. But what was a little risk compared to the potential rewards he tried to explain to Ryan as his countryman's face grew a shade darker with every detail of Kearney's plan laid out in front of him.

'Yous got a feckin' death wish or somtin'?' Ryan said finally.

'Aw, c'mon man. There might be a smidge of risk but it's not like going after a mad lion with a penknife or something. Get this right and we'll be back to the auld sod ordering drinks all round in no time.'

Ryan just sat there staring at his bottle. After what Kearney had told him, it sounded like the lion hunt was by far the safer option.

'Look,' said Kearney trying to sound reassuring, 'it's not as if they even found it and the fact that they didn't is a gift to people like you and me. There's not many who know the bush better and all we have to do is locate it and sell the information to them.'

'Locate it, is it?' said Ryan with a sneer. 'Does yous know hows many's tried and either failed or never been seen again?'

'I know,' said Kearney. 'But this is too good an opportunity to miss. These blokes were on to something. I know it. They weren't the types to do a trip like that without good reason. They must've got a sniff of where it is and I'd bet the Falcon they'd pay big bucks to narrow the search down.

'All I'm saying is that we work out some way of getting the information they want and sell it to them. I'm not saying we should go get it ourselves. They can do that. That's where the real death wish part of it is.'

'Yous feckin' joshin' me? Even passing on a hint of where it's at would be like dancin' wid der divil his self. Yous had som mad feckin' hare-brained ideas in yous time but dat's der maddest feckin' hare-brained ting dat's ever come outer yous mouth. Only a real desperate eejit would get involved in der hunt for red feckin' mercury.'

chapter twenty-two

Maybe he did have a death wish, thought Kearney. Maybe Ryan was right. Was that why he'd washed up in Africa in the first place? If ever there was a place that seemed designed to kill you it was what the Victorian explorers called the white man's grave.

Did they have a death wish too? They weren't ignorant of Africa's reputation. Yet they'd still flocked to the dark continent all looking for the same thing Kearney was looking for – a way to get off it with their pockets full.

But was that all of it? Was it just about making their fortunes? No, Kearney decided. There was definitely something more. He was realising that now.

Deep down he knew that the real motivation behind his wanderlust into places and situations no sane person would venture lay in one word – freedom. Freedom, he was now admitting to himself, from being locked for life into a brain-withering job he both despised and detested for the sole purpose of paying off a crippling mortgage to keep a nagging wife and brats happy.

The very thought of it made Kearney wince. That's where the real death wish was. It'd be like being locked in a dark cell was to that poor Kalahari bushman in 'The Gods Must Be Crazy'.

It was a film Kearney often reflected on. Especially that scene. Every time he thought about it he as good as wept. With such a strong affinity to someone with no conception of either walls or doors he could imagine what the bushman was going through. Purgatory.

Yet despite the affinity he felt for the bushman something still nagged. What was it?

It had taken until his ride on the Kenya Railway's boneshaker for enlightenment to dawn.

Despite their similarities, Kearney had realised there was one major difference between them. While the bushman needed nothing 'civilisation' could offer, Kearney's conditioning made him a slave to the material world. Unlike the bushman, he was wedded to the internal combustion engine, refrigeration and drinks that came in bottles – large dark brown ones preferably – and for all of these things you needed something the bushman didn't.

Cash in sufficient quantities, Kearney's ride on the train made him finally admit, was the only thing that would really set him free. He was no monk or bushman. Without a decent stash he'd never escape the gravitational pull of being beholden to others, never get off the treadmill, never be able to order a drink without first fingering the coins in his pocket.

His freedom was in that long sought-after pot of gold. He realised that now. But how to lay his hands on it? That was the question that had bugged him up until he'd boarded the Mombasa Express.

Then… PING! Enlightenment number two. There it was. It was right within his grasp. Freedom beckoned and all thanks to Kenya Railways, the Chinese, Beatrice Kinyui and, not insignificantly, a former girlfriend in Hong Kong.

*　*　*

When enlightenment came, it came with such a jolt it left Kearney straining at the chains round his wrists to punch the air in triumph, dance a jig of delight around the compartment and startle the train's comatose conductor almost into consciousness.

'JAYZUZ FOCKIN' CHRIST,' yelped the conductor's prisoner. 'That's fockin' it! We use the barter system. That way there's no money trail left to lead the bastards back to us!'

The key to it all lay in a former problem Kearney was now viewing as a positive blessing. Thanks to his brush with Beatrice Kinyui he now had a way in. A somewhat risky way, no doubt about it, but what was life without a little risk? If he hadn't risked his whole career on taking that first job with an oil exploration outfit no one had ever heard of on a continent he knew virtually nothing about, he'd never have had half the fun he had had and he wouldn't now be on the verge of pulling off a coup that could see him safe home with riches in abundance and more arriving every day as subscriptions to his African solar electrification scheme poured in.

Everything hinged on Kinyui believing he'd do what he intended to tell her he'd do – pre-empt the inevitable and deliver news of their dalliance direct to her husband before the bush telegraph blew the whole thing out of proportion and him out of the water with it.

Although such an act of atonement was the last thing on his mind, Kearney was prepared to bet that Kinyui wouldn't dare call his bluff. Being as aware as anyone that Africa was a man's world, Kinyui would know that such acts of penitence from one man to another could well find a sympathetic ear leaving most of the bill for an indiscretion in the lap of the unfortunate female. The gamble was that Kinyui would do almost anything to avoid having to pay it.

But Kearney wasn't after just any old thing. His wish list was far more specific. His partner in sexual crime held the key to the door currently standing between him and the next stage of his scheme to make China a willing collaborator in his solar project

– the name of the man in charge of Kenya's stockpile of confiscated animal parts.

That name was the last link in the chain of an idea that had started forming in Kearney's mind the moment he'd frozen while doing up his fly in the bushes at the Lake Baringo camp.

It wasn't that Kearney planned to earwig Xi's conversation with the camp's water boy. It's just the way it had turned out.

'JAYzus,' he exclaimed to himself. 'The fockers. Dragging me up here on a false pretext. They're not interested in mythical nightjars. They're after the cherry on the fockin' cake!'

Colour-wise it was a fairly apt allusion except that cherries on cakes were decidedly more plentiful than the fabled red mercury. Although many had heard of it, no one Kearney had ever met on his travels had ever convinced him they'd actually seen any.

Like mermaids, unicorns and the yeti, red mercury was the stuff of legend dreamers in bars mooned over, imagining what they'd do with the millions they could get for just a few bottles of the stuff. Word was that just one bottle full – preferably one of the old, now obsolete, Treetop fruit squash bottles because of the tensile strength of the bottle's cannon shell shape – could get you a six-figure sum in dollars.

It wasn't just the material's rarity that gave it its value, went the bar room gossip. It was the extra bang you could get for your buck when red mercury was incorporated in a nuclear weapon. Hence the triple-lock razor wire secrecy surrounding its alleged existence and location, forced on Kenya by the country's western aid donors so the story went.

If Kenya wanted to stay on the aid recipient list, and if the ministers who'd been ripping the aid money off wanted to avoid seeing the names of their Swiss bank accounts leaked into the public domain, all they had to do was keep undesirable elements from unearthing the red mercury secret.

As Kearney bedded down for his final night at Lake Baringo, his mind had taken off on a safari of its own. Somewhere in what he'd heard was a way to not only recoup his unexpected outlay on the hotel at Lake Turkana but to recoup it with interest, a lot of interest. The question was, how?

With the answer eluding him, Kearney eventually drifted off certain it'd present itself in the morning. When it hadn't, Kearney was plunged into a two-week ordeal of mind-wracking that left him no closer to cracking the code than he'd been at Lake Baringo.

The only thing he knew for certain was that even if he did know the location of the fabled substance he couldn't just sell it to the Chinese. The stink such a dirty transaction would generate would be picked up by the secret service bloodhounds in minutes and if he escaped being renditioned to a place or places unknown minutes afterwards, he'd be counting himself a very lucky man.

So no, a simple sale was out of the question and right up to the moment Kearney boarded the Mombasa Express he was still struggling for an alternative.

Then he remembered Kinyui and suddenly a bulb lit up in his head. With her help, voluntary or not, he had the basis of a plan that would not only see him fulfil a long-held dream but fulfilling it at the expense of Africa's latest colonial wannabe and all without any evidence linking him to the 'crime'. It was all too perfect.

* * *

It was all the staring out of the compartment's grimy window at the star-lit African bush that'd started the train of thought.

'Lucky bastards,' thought Kearney, imagining all the wildlife frolicking around out there while he was shackled to the seat of a travelling death trap. 'How nice to be an elephant with nothing on your mind other than losing both it and the rest of the herd in the twilight of your days. Wandering around lost with no one to help until you eventually keeled over and died of thirst wouldn't be nice. Not nice at all.'

Kearney assumed such keelings-over happened a lot. So why, he mused, wasn't the bush littered with the carcases of elephants whose lives had run their natural course. In all his years in Africa he'd seen only a few. Lots of middle-aged ones slaughtered for their tusks but hardly any that still had the tusks attached. Weird.

But not so weird when you thought about it. With ivory so highly prized in the East and poaching so rampant, it'd be a very lucky elephant who made it to its dotage. Likewise with rhino, lion, cheetah, leopard and even the humble giraffe, every one of them a poaching target and every loss another nail in the coffin of safari tour guides like himself.

It was something that dominated the conversation whenever the paths of the safari bwanas crossed. Without something to show to camera-touting tourists, it wasn't just the animals on the endangered species list. No wildlife to show the tourists meant cancelled bookings and no bookings meant no tour guide contracts.

That day hadn't dawned yet but Kearney and his mates could see it coming and there wasn't a man jack amongst them who wasn't looking for alternative employment.

No one would ever describe Kearney and Ryan as sentimental softies but when it came to preserving Africa's wildlife they were willing to make an exception. Apart from Africa just not being Africa without its abundance of wild animals, they had a business to run, one specialising in getting closer to the big five than anyone else.

In the early days of working the safari business, it was mostly Americans, Japanese and West Europeans taking up Kearney's challenge to 'get close enough to smell the beast's breath'. These days it was the Chinese.

When Africa first had the pleasure of welcoming Kearney and Ryan to its shores in 1989 people of Chinese origin on the continent were outnumbered ten to one by the rhino. A quarter of a century later, that ratio had not only reversed but increased massively thanks, in no small part, to the interest the one had in the other. The more the Chinese population in Africa swelled – to over a million by the time Kearney experienced the first of his tie rod breaks – the sharper the decline in rhino and other big game numbers in the wild. It was a coincidence that had not gone unnoticed by those with an interest in preserving the region's wildlife, Kearney and Ryan amongst them.

But what could they do about it? Neither anti-poaching measures nor education seemed to be working. Thanks to the Chinese in particular, the raw material on which the safari operators depended was running critically low and there seemed nothing to be done except look for alternative means of making ends meet.

* * *

It was while Kearney was trawling the internet for something – anything – that might fit the employment bill that he came across it. Something about the poaching problem had long niggled at him and it was while he was poring over the websites of organisations devoted to countering it that he discovered the reason. The sums didn't add up.

Kearney's long hours in front of the computer had thrown up two conflicting pieces of information. While it was undeniable that big game numbers in the region were falling, prices for their parts on the East Asian markets had yet to go through the roof. Why? As anyone with even the most rudimentary understanding of supply/demand economics knew, prices should rise when commodity shortages left suppliers unable to satisfy their customers' requirements.

But there it was in black and white. He had it from the horse's mouth, a former girlfriend who'd dumped him following his attempt to emulate the animals she'd confessed she preferred to his company and who'd ended up dedicating herself with almost nun-like devotion to the work of a Hong Kong-based animal rights organisation.

The girlfriend, impressed by his espoused road to Damascus conversion to the cause, had not only answered his email asking for confirmation of the figures but had gone several steps further. Yes, she'd said, not only were the prices he'd found accurate but that she had proof. Would he be interested in seeing a secretly-filmed meeting between a Sikh gentleman and two of her organisation's Chinese members masquerading as buyers of illicit animal parts?

The video confirmed two things in Kearney's mind. One, that prices were stable. The figures being quoted by the Sikh verified it. Two, that the trade wasn't the sole preserve of shady criminal gangs. The Sikh conducting the negotiation was a well-known figure in high Nairobi circles.

Putting the two together Kearney could hardly believe the picture that was forming in his head. If prices were stable, that meant supply was too. But Kenya in particular had been trumpeting the success of its anti-poaching programme. The two didn't match up.

Or they didn't until Kearney switched to conspiracy mode. If supply was stable, there could be only one reason. Demand was being satisfied from stock and there was only one stock big enough to satisfy the appetite of the likes of the Chinese. It had to be coming from the stash of animal parts the Kenyan authorities had confiscated from big game poachers and were, for reasons unexplained, keeping under lock and key rather than burning.

Sure there'd been a few well-publicised bonfires of elephant tusks to trumpet Kenya's sincerity when it came to cracking down on poaching. But as everyone in the safari game knew, that was just a token. Judging by the ever-dwindling numbers of game in the wild and the ever-increasing rumours of vast quantities of parts being secretly taken into custody by the Kenya Wildlife Service, somewhere there had to be warehouses full of the stuff. Unless, of course, it was being diverted east along some sort of Silk Road in reverse.

Although the video couldn't prove the stock was ending up in China, the two 'buyers' just role-playing for the undercover film, it did throw up something about this particular trade that had Kearney running and re-running the video several times. His focus wasn't on the Sikh, someone Kearney could instantly put a name to, but on an unspeaking and unidentified African man hovering in the background, a man clearly not one of the Sikh's muscle-bound henchmen.

As hard as he scrutinised the video and the blown-up print-outs of the African, Kearney was at a loss to place him. Having been a player in the safari game for the better part of twenty years, Kearney knew most of Kenya's 'names' by sight at least. But this man eluded him and in the end he'd been forced to admit defeat to the girlfriend who'd told him the African's identity was central to her organisation's ability to pursue the matter further. They didn't want to go off half-cock. Unless they could put names to all involved, they'd have to put the video on ice.

As much as Kearney would have liked to see the Sikh get his comeuppance, he understood his girlfriend's reluctance to splash the news before her organisation had the whole story. He too wanted all involved netted and pilloried. His business and, he secretly admitted to himself, his chances of making amends with a woman he still fantasised about, depended on putting such men out of circulation. Which was why he decided to keep the print-out with him at all times in case he ever came across someone looking like the man his nose was telling him was one of Kenya's best kept secrets.

Despite all his years working with Kenya's safari industry and, by association, with the Kenya Wildlife Service, never had the name of the man in charge of Kenya's animal parts stockpile so much as been alluded to. If anyone did know they weren't saying and there was a very good reason for the secrecy. If ever it became public it'd make him a marked man. He'd be a coercion target without peer in the eyes of both the poachers and those who stood to make millions from plundering the horde.

The more he'd looked at the print-outs of the man in the video, the more Kearney's suspicions grew. Could it be? If it was, what was such a man doing at a furtive meeting between sellers and buyers of animal parts?

In spite of all his other preoccupations, the man's face haunted Kearney, keeping him vigilant and alert for the next two years. But with no one resembling the man crossing his path, even such an all-enveloping obsession was beginning to fade and Kearney had all but given up hope of ever knowing the answer.

But then had come Beatrice Kinyui, sex goddess, impetuous adulterer and high ranking Kenya Wildlife Service official, and that interest had sparked vigorously back into life. If with her 'help' he could match the picture with a man who should be the last person involved in the illicit sale of animal parts to the Chinese, not only would he and Ryan be within touching distance of that long sought-after treasure trove but maybe, just maybe, his ex-girlfriend could be enticed out of her nunnery.

chapter twenty-three

For once in his life Ryan was struck dumb. Sitting there listening to Kearney's next great money-making wheeze, the only evidence he showed of following the plot was his gradually widening eyes. By the time Kearney had finished, they were twin full moons.

'So let me get dis straight,' Ryan managed once all had been revealed. 'Yous wants me to help yous blackmail not one but two high-up government officials to get a map o' de location o' prob'ly der most secret material in der world so's yous can trade it to China's version o' der mafia in return for a few bits o' technology yous could get in an a'ternoon off any hooky trader down Tom Mboya Street. Dat about roight?'

'They're not just any old bits of technology,' countered Kearney defensively. 'They're the key to making the whole scheme work. I'm after the best the Chinese can produce and I'm after a lot of it and all for nothing. Unless the system is reliable, we'll be spending more time repairing it than the income stream is worth.'

'But der blackmail bit is roight, roight?'

'Incentivisation.'

'Yous can call it what yous feckin' loike but yous still plannin' to put der squeeze on two o' der best connected people in bleddy Kenya unless dey plays der game accordin' to Kearney's feckin' rules. Dat's not only blackmail, it's a one-way ticket to der feckin' mortuary!'

Kearney could see the point but waved it away.

'There's a bit of a risk, I'll grant you that. But this is too good an opportunity to miss. It could finally be our ticket out of here.

'Anyway, chances are it'll fall on its arse at the first hurdle. Kinyui will probably call my bluff and tell me to piss off. But we've got to try something. We've been on this continent so long we're becoming choc-ices in reverse. I dunno about you but I've reached the point at which I'd do almost anything to sample a pint o' the black stuff again. Anyway, think of the craic that's in it.'

Kearney knew by the look on Ryan's face that his final shot had left his countryman snookered behind the black. No full-bloodied Irishman could ever turn down the chance of a laugh and a joke, especially if it involved substantial quantities of good Irish stout. To do so was seen as tantamount to treason. There was the national reputation to consider.

'Yous a feckin' eejit wid a feckin' eejit of a plan,' grumbled Ryan knowing Kearney had him by the balls. 'But since yous seems dead set on getting youssell disembowelled,' he added with a meaningful look into Kearney's smiling eye, 'yous gives me no choice but to be around when dat happens. Someone's gotta pick up der pieces an' ship 'em back to de auld sod. Anyway, half o' dat pot o' gold is moine.'

* * *

By the end of their drinking session Kearney had filled in all the gaps and outlined Ryan's required participation in the plan.

'Mostly I'll need you in a support role,' Kearney told him. 'As back-up, so-to-speak.'

'Yous means muscle,' Ryan said.

'No Ryan, most definitely not that. There's to be no strong-arm tactics. Just another... presence... on occasion to help all involved get the message.'

'Roight. Muscle it is den.'

Kearney gave up. If Ryan wanted to be seen as Kearney's tame persuader, so be it. Nothing was going to convince him otherwise. But since he'd never make a move without Kearney's say-so, Kearney felt pretty confident of coming through it without having to lift a finger against anyone, especially a woman. If Kinyui was going to be persuaded to cooperate it'd be by guile, not by the look on Ryan's face. In any case, Kearney reckoned that part of the plan would be the most straightforward. There wasn't a woman in Africa who didn't know the price of an indiscretion uncovered.

With Kinyui all but in the bag, provided the man in the video was the stockpile man, Kearney could then move on to the difficult part – cornering him and getting him to agree to both locate and part with official documents on the source of red mercury. This, Kearney knew, would take careful handling, starting with showing him a series of print-outs from his ex-girlfriend's video. That should at least focus his mind into giving Kearney's 'request' more than cursory consideration.

'An' if he comes up wid some reason why he can't get der information? What den?'

'That's where you come in. If he tries to fob us off with something like it being above his pay-grade, it's your job to help him reappraise his position. A simple reminder that he'll have no pay-grade at all if the video gets into the public domain should be enough. And no rough stuff. That understood?'

Ryan looked downcast. Not well versed in the art of making a point with words alone, all he could think of to do in the face of Kearney's command was to take a long hard pull on his bottle. When he'd done, he emerged with a twinkle in his eye.

'An' if he still won't cooperate?' he said with a crooked smile.

'Then we're done. We walk away knowing we've done our best

but it just wasn't good enough. With something like this it's best not to lose sight of your limitations.'

'But your man will know what we's a'ter,' said Ryan, the disappointment of being denied just the odd tap or two replacing the smile on his face. 'Surely he'll just pass dat on to der Garda an' den where'll we be?'

'You're forgetting the video,' countered Kearney. 'That's our ace in the hole. While we've got that I'd put money on him going nowhere near the police. If he did he knows what the outcome would be and I'd lay odds that he'd risk doing what we want rather than be fingered for being an accomplice in a scheme to divert animal parts to China. It might take some time for the penny to drop but I reckon he'll see sense in the end.'

'An' if he don't?'

'Like I said, that's when we walk away… fast.

'But just suppose he can and will get it,' said Kearney dreamily. 'Think of what we'll be able to do with it. We'll be able to wrap the Chinese around our little fingers. I'd wager they'd pay anything to know what we'd know.'

At the mention of the promise of untold riches Ryan's face brightened but then darkened again as Kearney unravelled the rest of the plan. Especially the bit about demanding stuff rather than money – the bit Kearney considered the genius part of the whole enterprise.

'No feckin' money?' Ryan exploded. 'But dat's de one ting we DO feckin' want. What yous planning to take instead, feckin' chopsticks?'

'Technology,' said Kearney. 'That's the key to this whole thing. If we barter the information for stuff rather than cash there's far less likelihood of leaving footprints. If anyone asks, with the right paperwork we can show it's a straight import deal.'

'Wadderyermean, if anyone asks? Yous seriously tink no one's going to wonder about der Choinese laying hands on someting dat'd put dem roight up der wid der nuclear superpowers a'ter being seen talkin' to a couple o' feckin' Oirishmen!'

Kearney smiled into his drink. 'But that's just it. Even if they did suspect a connection they'd never be able to prove it. The only link that'll exist between us and the Chinese will be a contract for the regular supply of solar panels and air compressors. The security goons will never think to look for something so anodyne. They'll be looking for a money trail. One they'll never find cos it simply won't exist.'

While Ryan was trying to work out the meaning of the word anodyne, Kearney had moved on. The beauty of the plan, he crowed, lay in its very longevity, another word Kearney could see Ryan struggling with.

'To ensure supplies for the solar scheme don't get disrupted before everything's up and running and earning money, since we'll be the ones with the information we can give it to them bit by bit. Not the location of any actual finds. Just directions to where the government men have been digging. Once they'd got that they can go and see for themselves.

'But since I'll be making sure they don't look in the prime locations right off, I think I can guarantee a fairly long and profitable relationship between us and our visitors from the Orient. I think it's what the Chinese call a win-win situation.'

* * *

With Ryan eventually grudgingly admitting to seeing the method in Kearney's madness, Kearney slept well that night. Not just because he now had someone he could trust to watch his back but because he'd managed to convince himself that his hands, though not clean exactly, were at least well-manicured.

Win-win seemed to sum the situation up exactly. Or, since the Chinese would be getting two for the price of one, even win-win-win, thought Kearney hoping that wouldn't sound too Irish to someone not from the Emerald Isle.

The Chinese would not only be getting a lead into acquiring something they'd long-cherished but also a potential new market for all the solar panels they were producing and couldn't sell. Meanwhile, he and Ryan would be getting supplies of something that'd make them rich at no cost to themselves. It was beauty personified.

Well, it was if you discounted the treachery thing.

Kearney wasn't blind to the fact that, in the eyes of some, even being suspected of helping the Chinese get red mercury would put him right up there with AQ Khan, the Pakistani physicist who'd helped North Korea get the bomb.

Well, they can think what they like, thought Kearney as he dozed happily off. In his high-minded estimation, it was only right that balance existed between the global superpowers. If the West alone had a nuclear super-device, it'd put the rest of the world – and probably outer space too – at its mercy. Having seen what technological superiority by an outsider had done to Ireland in the past, Kearney had no desire to see a modern day repeat of that iniquitous state of affairs. To his mind, if there was going to be a fight, it had to be a fair fight and if he could play a part in ensuring it was, then that would be just fine. He could live with that.

* * *

He could also live with the guilt of knowing he hadn't provided his ex-girlfriend's organisation with everything he knew about the Kenya/China animal part smuggling operation. After due consideration, Kearney had come to the painful decision that it would hardly be in his immediate best interests to have the name of the man at the heart of the operation revealed to the world. That was his bargaining blue chip.

Anyway, for the moment at least, he was being honest. He didn't have a name to give her. That would only become an issue once he'd worked out how to go about approaching a woman he'd only recently had illicit sex with with an offer she couldn't refuse. Tricky wasn't the word.

For three days Kearney picked up the phone and replaced it without dialling. Get this wrong, he told himself, and there was every chance of her refusing point-blank to cooperate, slamming the receiver down incandescent with rage. That'd be as bad as her calling his bluff. He could hardly go through with the threat of approaching her husband direct. Apart from the little matter of not knowing who he was, trusting an African man to show understanding when approached with a request for clemency for shagging his wife would be about as sensible as trusting Ryan to look after his drink.

So, only after rehearsing making the call a million times, Kearney trying to predict every permutation as to how the conversation might go, did he hesitantly lift the receiver and dial, beads of sweat trickling down his temples.

'*Habari*. Beatrice Kinyui's office,' Kearney heard a voice he didn't recognise say.

Shitefockfockfockshite. Why the fock hadn't he rehearsed this bit? How the fock could he have been so stupid not to have foreseen that Kinyui's calls were likely to go through a bloody secretary? Fockin' eejit. Ryan was right. He wasn't cut out for such shenanigans.

For a moment he froze. Then he panicked.

'Solly. Long number,' was all he could think of saying, hoping the pantomime Chinese accent would lend credibility to the performance.

'Shite. Now what?' he scolded himself, dropping a receiver that'd just turned red hot in his hand. Apart from anything else he might just have alerted all concerned to the fact that there was a Chinese connection in all this.

'Fockin' eejit!' he wailed, beating his sweating temples hard with his fists. 'This is going to take more thought than I fockin' thought.'

chapter twenty-four

'So,' said Kariuki, 'did you give it him?'

'Of course,' said Kinyui. 'But not without a fight. And not without having to bite my lip. Some restraint was needed to keep from laughing in his face when he said that now he had the name, none of what happened between us would be finding its way back to my husband. You'd have thought he might've checked I actually had a husband before blackmailing me.'

'But you DID restrain yourself I hope.'

'Rather well I thought. Had a good giggle about it afterwards but at the time I was all mortification and mercy pleading. The harder part was when he first accosted me in the street. When he jumped out at me like that I wasn't prepared for what he had to say.'

Kinyui had been wondering when Kearney would make his move and how he'd go about it. With nothing but her place of work, her position and her office phone number on the card she'd 'mislaid' in the Landrover, and all calls to her office being filtered by her secretary, it was unlikely that the first contact would be by phone. And since he'd surely want to avoid bumping into the husband he didn't know she didn't have, even if he did know where she lived there was no way he was going to show up at her home.

That left only a personal visit to her office and a Kinyui bracing herself for a tap on the shoulder every time she went in or out.

With none coming for two weeks after their Landrover

interlude, Kinyui had half started thinking she hadn't done a good enough job of luring Kearney into her web. But then, one evening as she walked towards her car, he'd popped up from behind another waving a handkerchief.

At first she thought he was surrendering, an initial impression that was to quickly dissipate as their conversation progressed.

The handkerchief, explained Kearney, was a prop designed both to get her attention and fool anyone watching into thinking he was returning something she'd dropped. He didn't want to give the impression that the two already knew one another.

How sweet, she'd thought. He's going all mediaeval and chivalrous on me to woo me back to his embrace.

'How wrong can you be?' she'd said on reporting back to Kariuki. 'The only thing mediaeval about his approach was the way he'd broached the subject of what he really wanted. It was like being hit with a club.'

At first, Kearney had been the embodiment of gentlemanliness, apologising profusely for surprising her, but then hadn't wasted any time moving on to his real reason for tracking her down. It wasn't her body he was after, he'd pretty much told her, it was her contacts.

Thanks, she'd thought. If that's the way you get a girl to cooperate in Ireland I'm not surprised there are so many sad old Irishmen left wifeless and alone in their bogside hovels.

Even so, she was secretly glad the re-encounter had passed so swiftly, Kearney simply stating his requirements and telling her he'd await her call. She had, as requested by Kariuki, been able to get a first inkling into what Kearney was up to and all without the need for further carnal gymnastics – something of a disappointment really.

* * *

Kinyui's reaction to Kearney's demands at that first meeting was a combination of speechless astonishment and histrionic fury. How DARE he even THINK she could be coerced into helping him get the name he was after. She was a professional woman with professional ethics and nothing he could threaten her with could induce her to act in such an underhand manner.

It wasn't altogether an act. She really was offended that anyone could assume she'd simply roll over and cooperate under duress. But as she ranted, she'd warmed to the wronged woman role even going so far as to try a slap in the face.

As she slammed her car door and roared off into the evening traffic she smiled to herself.

'Not bad,' she'd thought. 'I make quite a convincing woman scorned. It'll make the transformation to woman humbled equally as convincing when the time comes.'

Two days later, she'd decided that moment had arrived. After allowing just enough time to plant the thought in his mind that she was allowing her fury to dissipate, she'd called the number he'd scrawled on the handkerchief, softening her voice to tearful pussycat tones.

'PLEEEASE Kal! Please don't do it. You KNOW what'll happen to me. Can you live with that?'

Silence.

'You bastard,' she'd bleated, breaking down into theatrical tears. 'You men are all the same. You only want one thing.'

'Two, actually,' came Kearney's icy response. 'The first was nice but now we've moved on. It's time to pay for your moment of madness.'

'GOD! Were you planning this all along? Is that why you seduced me? Did it mean nothing to you?'

Silence.

More tears. Then finally, 'OK. I'll try.'

'Good move. Twenty-four hours enough for you?'

'More than enough,' thought Kinyui, softly replacing the receiver. 'I've got the name right here but I'm still going to make you sweat for it you son of a baboon's bottom. Don't want anyone smelling a rat by being over-obliging, do we?'

By the end of the next day Kearney had both the name and the man's room number in the KWS building, whispered to him by Kinyui as they pretended to go after the same bunch of bananas in a downtown supermarket.

'Good,' said Kearney's eyes. 'Now you can relax and forget we ever met.'

'Hope the bananas poison you,' Kinyui's told him in return.

* * *

Actually, I hope they don't, thought Kinyui on her way home to the house she shared with no one save her sizeable pet python. If they do, all this subterfuge and game-playing will have been for nothing.

Kariuki was thinking much the same thing. The last thing he wanted was for any mishap to befall the Irishman. Now he had some sort of insight into the direction Kearney's mind was travelling, he knew he'd never rest easy until he knew its final destination.

The permutations seemed endless. What could he be up to? And how did the Chinese he'd been doing safari work for fit into all this? Was he planning some sort of scam to get access to the animal parts stockpile and sell them on? If he was, he must have better contacts in the underworld than Kariuki thought. Getting the parts out of the stockpile and then out of Kenya would require a great deal more arranging than he suspected Kearney was capable of.

But what if he was just a foot soldier working on behalf of some well-oiled smuggling racket? That was far more likely. From the little he knew about Kearney, Kariuki wouldn't put it past him to go conveniently blind to the moral aspects of animal parts trafficking in pursuit of a sizeable payday.

Yes, that was more like it. But who could he be working for? It was unlikely to be one of the established smuggling rings. Kariuki knew most of the players involved, by and large high profile characters maintaining highly respectable outward images. And since all operations were exclusively either African or Asian-run, neither was ever likely to cross the racial divide and risk damaging their enterprises by entrusting operations to a *mzungu*, especially a chancer like Kearney.

The more he thought about it, if this was an animal parts smuggling operation it had to be a new one. With Oriental connections perhaps? Was that what was behind the Kearney/China relationship Moses had told him about? Were they colluding to smuggle the parts direct to China rather than go through the regular middleman channels?

If they were, thought Kariuki, Kearney was unwittingly providing an answer to not one but two of the things that left him sleepless at night – how to pay back the church 'loan' from the bank and how to get even with the Chinese for scamming him in Mombasa. If he didn't come up with the means of resolving both pretty soon, not only would he find himself ruined and destitute but deprived of a good night's sleep for ever.

The more Kariuki thought about what he now knew, the more he began sensing that the answer to both problems was being presented to him in a single package. If a Kearney/China animal parts smuggling racket was being planned and Kariuki could prove it, the thought of the divine retribution Kenya's established smuggling rings would bring down on the Chinese coupled with the gratitude they'd show for being made privy to the information made Kariuki's eyes shine. Few deals he was ever likely to cut would ever be as satisfying as this one. Could this be perfection personified? There was only one way to find out.

As much as he'd have liked to have started celebrating straight off, patience he knew was paramount. There'd be no onpassing of information and no popping of corks until his suspicions had been confirmed and the only way of doing that was to attach an extra shadow to the Irishman.

There was only one man for the job. The one who'd tipped Kariuki off about Kearney and the Chinese in the first place.

* * *

Moses left Kariuki's church office in high spirits. If there'd been any doubt before, now there was none. He truly was one of the chosen ones. Never before had he been entrusted with such responsibility and was determined not to let his pastor down. Anyway, he was intrigued. If Kearney was on Kariuki's radar, that made him a man of interest. His pastor never bothered himself with nonentities.

Three days later he was back in the church office bringing Kariuki up to date with Kearney's movements.

'Bwana Kearney spend much time in beer halls with another Ireland bwana, name of Ryan,' Moses reported.

'He also visit Kenya Wildlife Service building for some time then come out and wait in car I do not recognise. Not usual Landrover.

'Later, Kearney follow Africa man from KWS to Serena Hotel and catch man in car park. Even me, I do not know the Africa man but looks an important *mzee*.

'Very serious palaver follows and Africa man looking angry when Kearney showing him something. Then Africa man go hotel while Kearney go beer hall to meet with bwana Ryan and share much palaver and much Tusker at much cost. Much cost to me also, Pastor...'

'Understood,' said Kariuki handing Moses a five hundred shilling bill. 'This should cover your expenses.'

'*Asante sana, mzee.*'

'And there'll be same same for the next few days providing you bring me something new. Something of interest.'

Moses left the church enthused but troubled. Kariuki's request for him to stay on Kearney's tail was going to be a problem. His boss at the Chinese news agency also needed his services. He couldn't feign a debilitating bout of malaria forever. It was a job he didn't want to lose.

Then a brainwave. He could subcontract the Kearney-watching operation to his cousin Solomon. It would suit them both.

Without much work coming in at his garage in Ngong, out of embarrassment for being unable to contribute to the collection plate, Solomon had been missing services at the church both he and Moses attended. Unless that changed, Moses fretted that come the day of judgement they'd both be having to answer to a higher power. In accordance with the pastor's Good Samaritan teachings, Moses knew that if he declined to help his cousin in his hour of need, God might view him as one of the ones who'd passed by on the other side.

So Solomon it'd be. He had no option but to go to his cousin's assistance. And anyway, bwana Kearney might begin to suspect something if he started seeing Moses wherever he went.

* * *

Cousin Solomon had been only too pleased to lend a hand. Not only would it help him out of his financial hole but it'd be reasonably simple keeping tabs on a man he already knew and who had yet to help Solomon secure his place at the right hand of the Almighty.

If Kearney started suspecting he was being followed, Solomon could simply say he was concerned about Kearney's final destination come the end of days.

It wasn't a lie as such. Solomon really was concerned that the one he'd helped on the Ngong Road had yet to be seen at the Church of Our Saviour's Number One Good Samaritans. Until he was, Kearney risked facing eternal damnation and the heavenly kudos Solomon was owed for adding another member to the church's flock would remain unpaid.

In the end, no explanation for his presence was required. Kearney had pre-empted it by giving him short shrift when, on thinking he'd been rumbled, Solomon had boldly approached his target in a bid to circumvent any stalking accusation.

As he appeared at the table Kearney shared with the other Irishman in a dark corner of an Ngong shebeen, Kearney rapidly covered a piece of paper he and the other man were studying and told Solomon to kindly move away. But not in those exact words, he told Moses, and not before Solomon had glimpsed the contents of the paper. Under its Government of Kenya letterhead were the words 'red' and something else.

After first considering it unworthy of re-reporting to Kariuki Moses had had second thoughts. Kariuki had said to report back anything of interest. Kearney being secretive might fit the bill but only if he could get his cousin to expand on the contents of the paper.

'"Red" was most definitely one of the words but can't be sure of the other,' said Solomon. 'I think it might have begun with an "m".'

Pressed further by his cousin, Solomon screwed up his eyes and tried to visualise the document. Moments later he snapped his fingers. 'That's it. It was "m-e-something". Maybe the next letter was an "m" or an "n"' or an "r". It was difficult to see in that light with Kearney's hand over it.'

Despite his best efforts, Solomon had been unable to conjure anything more from his visual cortex leaving Moses no option but to report back a semi-finding to Kariuki, carefully skirting round the part his cousin had played in semi-finding it. The last thing he wanted was to incur the wrath of his pastor for farming the job out without permission and to risk being told to share the expenses fifty/fifty with his helper. Taking the lion's share was helping ease the pain of the news he'd just received from the Xinhua chief administrator.

Much to his surprise and consternation, Moses had been informed that his duties were being extended but not in the way he'd have liked. With Kearney now off the Xinhua 'filming' mission, Moses was now the team's navigator/driver.

The news left Moses some way short of outright elation. Apart from there being little extra money in it, there'd likely be no beer in the places they had to visit, he was being required to camp when they got there and, worst of all, there'd be scant opportunity of indulging in the sort of extracurricular activity he'd been enjoying with the chief administrator. Without that, there was every chance he'd start losing his manly appeal. It was the only exercise he got these days and he'd noticed her eye alighting on Moses' younger, slimmer, assistant at times.

It wasn't just the interludes with the chief administrator Moses would miss. It was the regular flow of expenses and the pastor's goodwill that went with the Kearney monitoring job. Unless Moses was in Nairobi to receive Solomon's reports and onpass them to Kariuki, they'd become as non-existent as his beer and extracurricular sex life.

For some days after receiving the news, Moses fretted over how to break it to his pastor. Depending on how he took it, Moses could well find himself leaving Kariuki's office stripped of his 'chosen one' status.

Finally, Moses could put the moment off no longer and was about to raise the issue with Kariuki when the pastor interrupted him with a request. One that not only laid Moses' worries to rest but handed him a readymade excuse for putting off making the going out of town announcement indefinitely.

'Moses,' Kariuki told him the day after Moses had relayed news of Kearney's secretive behaviour in the Ngong shebeen, 'on behalf of the church, I'd like to thank you most sincerely for all your valuable endeavours in the Kearney matter. They have not only been of immeasurable help in doing God's work but, like the loaves and fishes, with what you have brought me I'm confident the church will shortly be in a position to feed the five thousand.

'Your input has been a true godsend to both myself and the church and, as such, I hope the church can continue counting on your assistance. For I have to inform you that God Himself has ordained me to extend to you personally His plea that you carry out one more task in His name. He has decreed that you and only you are suited to undertake a mission that could well prove more taxing than the last and therefore of even more benefit to the church.

'Should you be willing to undertake it, Moses, God has assured me that you would not only be helping feed the five thousand but will be responsible for consigning to purgatory and eternal damnation an ungodly sinner and blasphemer of the highest order.

'Moses, God is asking you directly for help that you and only you can give. Many are called but few are chosen, Moses. Can you deny that call? Be sure that God will see in your heart any weakness in your spirit.'

'Well,' thought Moses, his mouth hanging agape on realising he was effectively being raised to apostolic status, 'since you put it like that, how can I refuse?'

Seeing the light of guaranteed redemption light up in Moses' eyes, Kariuki felt he had no need of waiting for an answer.

'You, Moses, are a man in the sight of God. Blessings will rain down on your head and you shall forever be counted amongst the righteous. For what He has to ask of you is not for the feint of heart or weak of spirit. Accomplish this task and be assured that a seat awaits at God's right hand. You have been chosen as the instrument of heaven, a sentinel of all that is holy. The Lord God is counting on you. Do not let Him down.

'Like your namesake receiving the tablets on Mount Sinai, you, Moses, are instructed to go forth and do the Lord's work. Starting with following the man Kearney into the wilderness.'

chapter twenty-five

No one was more surprised than Kearney when his plan started falling neatly into place. Well, no one except Ryan. This went so contrary to his countryman's track record that Ryan started suspecting Kearney was getting some help.

'O ye of little faith,' was Kearney's reaction. 'Think about it. Who the fock would help us? Certainly not Kinyui. She as much as spat in my face when I told her the price of my silence. I don't blame her actually. It was a pretty mean thing to do but I can live with it. Means to an end and all that.'

Ryan was neither convinced nor as confident as Kearney about how smoothly everything was going.

'Yous full o' shoite, Kearney. Yous is gettin' help from somewhere. Oi knows it. An' anyway, ain't yous fergettin' sometin'? What about stockpile man? He's der only one who knows what we's really a'ter. If oi were him I'd be tinkin' o' getting in on de action. Der'd be far more in it fer him dan from sellin' poxy animal parts.

'Oi knows what oi'd do in his position,' grinned Ryan with a malicious glint in his eye. 'Oi'd have made anudder copy o' dat map an' be goin' a'ter it meself. Or waitin' til yous turns someting up an' be makin' plans to relieve yous of it.'

'He wouldn't dare,' countered Kearney confidently. 'He knows that if anything happens to me – or anything in my possession – that video goes straight to the Press. He couldn't risk that happening.'

'But he must know dat even a'ter gettin' us der map dat dat threat still hangs over him,' said Ryan. 'He's got no guarantee dat yous still wouldn't do it.'

'Absolutely. But he also knows that the video is my insurance. Unless he's completely thick, he knows I'd want to hang on to it in case he welshes on us. Once it's out, it's out for good and I've no longer got any hold over him. He knows it and I know it and that's why I don't expect to be getting any trouble from him.'

'Didn't look loike dat when we foirst cornered him in der Carnivore car park.'

Ryan was referring to the look of pure unadulterated hatred in the man's eyes when, as arranged, he'd parked his car next to the one Kearney had got Ryan to borrow and found Ryan's demolition site face leering at him through the driver's window.

It was a face to prompt nervous twitches at the best of times. In the dark in one of the car park's furthest recesses away from prying eyes it was enough to make you redefine your definition of swamp creature.

Ryan could tell straight away that the man wasn't expecting a pincer movement. That he'd come hoping to get this resolved face-to-face with Kearney alone. Not with Kearney and something that looked like it'd stepped straight out of Mary Shelley's darkest imaginings.

At first the man had held his nerve, but when Kearney opened the man's passenger door and got in both Kearney and Ryan could feel him tense. Despite his icy outward image, here was a clearly dyed-in-the-wool office man not used to being in close proximity to two creatures who could easily be mistaken for those he was more used to seeing in bits in his warehouse.

* * *

It'd taken patience setting the trap the man had eventually fallen into, Kearney having to first lurk close to the man's office in the Kenya Wildlife Service building, photo of the suspect in hand, to make sure they were one and the same person.

Once sure they were, Kearney had then had to surreptitiously tail him and pounce, but only when certain his approach would seem to onlookers like a chance meeting between two men already well-acquainted.

The Serena Hotel car park was perfect and Kearney could hardly believe his luck when the man parked up, got out and started walking alone towards the hotel. Even more so when the man turned on being addressed from behind by the name Kearney had been given by Beatrice Kinyui.

Gotcha, thought Kearney, walking up to him smiling with his hand out. When the man took it, it remained took and before he started struggling to release it, Kearney had delivered his *coup de grâce*.

Staring at the picture Kearney thrust in front of him, the man's hand froze in Kearney's iron foundry grip. Then, as Kearney told him about the video from which the photo was culled and about the meeting he was being invited to attend if he wanted to prevent the video seeing the light of day, it went limp.

Kearney's first demand made no mention of red mercury. That, he'd decided, would come later. Instead, he'd decided to deliver his demands in bits, an appropriate way of going about things considering what it was the man was involved in trading to feather his filthy little nest. Anyway, it'd give the man time to get things straight in his head. To get over his initial shock and fury and see he really had little option but to cooperate.

First, Kearney told him, he'd be expecting to see him after dark the next evening in the car park of the Carnivore restaurant and nightclub, another appropriate Kearney choice considering what it was he was intending to do to the man if he didn't show up or if there was any indication that he hadn't come alone. In either case, Kearney told him, the video currently lodged in a safe place would be winging its way to every major media outlet in Kenya and the western world and the man could consider himself cooked meat.

Kearney hadn't been surprised that the man had arrived at the allotted place at the allotted time. He'd surely be assuming this to be nothing more than a money transacting sting and would want to get it over and done with without any undue delay.

His face on discovering it wasn't that simple was a picture that almost had Kearney laughing out loud. Both knew that wasn't how things were done in Kenya. Blaggers wanted cash not information. So when the man merely looked at Kearney, lower lip drooping as Kearney told him that all he had to do to get them off his back was to use his official standing to get them a copy of the government's investigations into the source of a specific mineral, Kearney nearly lost it. That simply did not compute.

It did when Kearney told him the name of the mineral. That's when the man's lip stopped drooping and started quivering.

'Yes,' thought Kearney, 'he HAS heard of red mercury.'

'But it doesn't exist,' stuttered the man. 'Everyone knows that. It's a myth.'

'Possibly. Possibly not. Either way, all I'm asking you to do is this one little thing for us. We KNOW the government's been looking for it. All we want to know is where. That's all. Get that for us and you're off the hook. You have my word that I won't be releasing that video.'

'And you'll be forgetting my name?'

Blimey, thought Kearney, that was bold. The little shite is daring to negotiate. Maybe he's not as limp-wristed as I'd thought.

'Of course,' said Kearney with as much conviction as he could muster. 'If your name ever gets out, be assured it won't be coming from me.'

* * *

On the way back to Ngong, Ryan was apoplectic.

'Yous a feckin' lyin' hypocrite, Kearney.'

'How's that then?'

'Tellin' the little shoyt you'd forget you ever heard of him or his shitty little operation. Dat's a big feckin' lie. Der foirst ting yous'll be doin' is spreadin' dat name all over bleddy Kenya. Tell me yous won't. Yous knows as well as me dat we's got ter put a stop to his little game if der big game is goin' ter survive,' said Ryan without realising he'd just made something equating to a joke.

'That's quite good,' said Kearney smiling. 'I like that.'

'What?'

'Your joke. I like it.'

'Oi'm not feckin' jokin'. Someting's gotta be done 'bout mister feckin' animal man. Der future of der whole feckin' safari game depends on it. Oh… roight… game… roight. Haha.

'But oi'm feckin' serious, Kearney. Yous can't be tinkin' of just droppin' it. Der's lives and livelihoods at stake here!'

'Why you little sentimentalist! Never had you down for an animal fundamental rights-ist. Not with that stash of ostrich bones you've got salted away. Who's the hypocrite now?'

'Go shoyt! Yous knows what oi'm tarkin' 'bout. It's 'bout not lettin' your bleddy mates down. Yous and me will be doin' grand out of it, sittin' pretty wid all dat dough comin' in from der solar scheme. But what 'bout de udder blokes. No feckin' animals means no feckin' tourists and no feckin' tourists means no feckin' business.'

'Course I know what you're talking about. I haven't forgotten the other boys. How could I? We're one big unruly family us safari bwanas. One big unruly family I'm not about to shite on. It's the only real family I've ever had. Stand on me. I'll see them right.'

'How? Dey'll be outta feckin' business!'

'Not necessarily. I only said the name wouldn't be coming from me. Didn't say anything about you… or the folks I got the video from.'

* * *

Two days later and Kearney had set the rendezvous point – the check-in hall at Wilson airport, another appropriate setting he thought. The smaller of Nairobi's two airports was the hub of the *miraa* trafficking trade to Somalia and no one there would look twice at two men poring over a set of papers and a map in the corner. They'd be too busy making sure no one was getting a glance at their own.

In the end there was to be no lengthy poring session. Just a cursory glance at the papers by Kearney to make sure they were what he hoped they'd be. Kearney was pretty sure they would. The man would know what would happen if Kearney discovered they were a fob-off.

Satisfied he'd got what he was after, Kearney turned, beckoned to Ryan loitering near the vending machine and left the man sitting, refusing to meet the eye of his nemesis.

Kearney could sense what was going through his mind. The man also knew what would happen if he was ever fingered for leaking the documents. But what could he do? The devil lay one way, a bloody great expanse of rough, open water the other.

But at least Kearney hadn't asked how he came by them, Kearney could almost hear him thinking. The Irishman seemed not to want to know. To him it seemed irrelevant.

Not to the animal parts man it wasn't. He'd taken a mighty big risk to get them and all he could hope was that the men at the Ministry of Defence were too dense to put two and two together.

While the man from the KWS fretted, Kearney and Ryan drank to the success of the project. Scrutinising the papers and map lying open on the table of the darkest alcove of one of Ngong Town's less comely establishments, it was clear that what lay in front of them was their passport out of Africa and back to the land of their births. If the Chinese didn't go for their suggested trade of information for technology they'd eat the Irish flag, sick it up over the Blarney Stone and openly declare that leprechauns were as mythical as the mineral they were after.

As they pored over the map, both felt fully confident it wouldn't come to that. Well, it wouldn't unless that bloody mechanic who'd staggered over to their table was more literate than he looked. If the man had been able to read what they were looking at, they might find themselves involved in another blackmail scam. On the wrong end of it.

Kearney felt certain of avoiding such an eventuality. Sensing the man's looming presence, he'd had the presence of mind to swiftly cover the key words with his hand. So even if the man had seen the Kenya government letterhead he wouldn't know what the content was.

In any case, the man Kearney didn't immediately recognise in the dim light of the bar not only looked ill-educated but three-fifths cut. If there were any repercussions, he told himself but not Ryan, he'd not only do the flag-eating, sicking up and leprechaun existence mockery things but would add lucky shamrock denial into the bargain.

'Ach,' thought Kearney, finally placing where he'd seen the man before and trying valiantly to exorcise any concern from his mind, 'nothing to worry about. Like all religious zealots they're more sheep than human. The only thing they can read is the one book and I don't remember any references to red mercury in any of the bible chapters I was forced to learn.'

So no, he told Ryan, no need to go to Plan B yet.

'What's Plan B?' said Ryan, fully aware that along with moderation, prudence and discretion, contingency planning, emergency exits and safety nets weren't wholly integral to the Irish character.

'Good point. Not sure there is one. Now we've got these papers we're past the point of no return. We're in it for good now, me bucko. So I'd say it's time for a toast.'

And with that Kearney raised his bottle and issued the pair's adopted war cry.

'*Hakuna wa fungwa*!'

'*Hakuna wa fungwa* to you too, yous feckin' eejit,' said Ryan clinking bottles with his countryman. 'No prisoners... on either side, oi feckin' hope.'

chapter twenty-six

No prisoners was exactly what was going through Gideon Kariuki's mind too. Now he knew what Kearney and Ryan were after, there'd be no room for pity. Now it was all or nothing with the Irish pair on the nothing side if Kariuki had anything to do with it.

Over and over, Kariuki went through his plan to make sure he hadn't missed anything. All the bases seemed covered. But still something nagged. What was it?

With nothing coming, once again Kariuki replayed the events of the past few days in his mind. After following Kearney to KWS headquarters, Moses had told him he'd seen the Irishman emerge some time later and had then followed him to the Serena Hotel. There he'd seen him meet with an African man in the car park and show the man something.

A day later, he'd followed Kearney again, this time at night to the Carnivore where Kearney had parked up and got into the car of what Moses thought was the same African man while Ryan skulked beside the driver's window.

Two days after that Moses had trailed Kearney and Ryan to Wilson airport and seen Kearney and that same African man looking at some papers the man had brought with him. Then Kearney had driven off with Ryan and the papers while the African sat with his head in his hands in the check-in hall.

Leaving the African man to fret over whatever it was he was fretting about, Moses had followed Kearney and Ryan to a bar in

Ngong Town and it was there that the secret had partly unfolded. The papers were official documents about something to do with red something.

It was that something that held the key, Kariuki was sure of it, not least because of what he knew of the African man's movements over the past few days.

Being nothing if not stringent in his planning, it wasn't just Kearney Kariuki had had followed. After learning the identity of the African man from Beatrice Kinyui, Kariuki knew he'd learn as much about what Kearney was playing at from the movements of this man as he would from attaching a shadow to Kearney.

Kariuki had the very man for the job, a police inspector who owed Kariuki a favour he could hardly get out of paying. The inspector had Kariuki to thank for being 'understanding' in the matter of a ghost bank account he needed to set up to accommodate funds accruing from police work that went 'beyond the call of duty', as he'd put it to Kariuki.

Despite the inspector's disdain at being asked to do something he normally got his minions to do, he'd grudgingly agreed to Kariuki's demand and had shadowed the KWS target Kariuki had identified.

The inspector's reports showed the man's movements coincided precisely with reports Kariuki was getting from Moses but with one major addition. In between the meeting with Kearney at the Carnivore and again at Wilson airport, the man had made a visit to the records office of the Ministry of Defence. Here, the inspector later discovered on using his position to inspect the records office sign-in book for the day, the man had requested general browsing access to papers in the ministry's scientific research section.

Between the man's lengthy visit to the ministry and the inspector's return to inspect the sign-in book, the inspector had followed the man to Wilson airport where he'd seen him meet with a large hairy *mzungu* and hand over some papers which the foreigner had glanced through before leaving.

'The target,' the inspector reported to Kariuki, 'remained in the check-in hall in what I would describe as a pensive state for some minutes after his meeting with the *mzungu* and then drove home where he stayed for the rest of the night.'

'Thank you,' said Kariuki. 'I think for the moment your mission is accomplished. However, I would be most grateful if you'd hold yourself in readiness should the need arise to resume monitoring activities.'

The inspector knew precisely what that meant. If he didn't drop everything to answer any call Kariuki felt like making on his time, he'd pretty soon be having to answer a rather more awkward call from a somewhat less civil superintendent of police.

* * *

Kariuki was no Fields medal mathematics scholar but he did have a numbers brain. He'd never have reached his current position in the bank without one. So, with two and two not beyond him, when he put the inspector's report of the KWS man's visit to the MoD together with Moses' report of what it was Kearney was looking at in the Ngong bar, Kariuki's arithmetic circuitry clicked into gear.

There was no doubt that Kearney was now in possession of whatever it was the KWS man had obtained from the MoD. There was also no doubt that it contained a map and that the map's title included the word 'red'.

But red what? All Kariuki had to go on was Moses' report that the other word's first two letters were 'm' and 'e' and that the third could be either 'm' or 'n' or 'r'.

Kariuki wracked his brain for a word with one of these three letters coming after the first two that went with the adjective 'red'. Memory? Menopause? Mercenary? Nothing seemed to fit.

Then, just as he was about to give up and turn in for the night, a thought. What would come up in the suggestion list if he typed the three combinations of letters into the Google search box? In an almost throwaway act of desperation, Kariuki gave it a go.

He was glad he did. After getting and discarding meme, membership, membrane, men, menu and menace, typing 'r' after the 'me' threw up something altogether more interesting. Not the first two – mermaid and Mercedes – but the third.

Kariuki beat his head with his fists. Why hadn't he thought of it straight off? It was so obvious when it was put in front of you and you recalled where it was the KWS man had been between meetings with Kearney at the Carnivore and Wilson airport. Even more obvious when you factored in who it was you were dealing with. If there was a bigger maverick than Kearney in Kenya, Kariuki had yet to come across him.

To a man like Kearney, the little matter of red mercury not only being a mythical substance but a closely-guarded state secret would be seen as more of a challenge than either a warning or a wild goose chase. If such a man got even the mildest of sniffs as to where red mercury might be found, he'd go after it like a hyena. He'd have no compunction about treading on any toe that got in the way of uncovering the secret… and of profiting handsomely from the find. Kariuki was as aware as anyone of the intrinsic value of the substance. And of the interest any number of people had in obtaining it… up to and including the Chinese. Were they the buyer Kearney was targeting? Kariuki wouldn't put it past him.

As Kariuki turned out the light and tried to sleep, alternate thoughts coursed through his brain. While two and two most definitely made four, they might not if you factored in wishful thinking. Allow that to interfere with a scientific calculation and you could well end up chasing your own tail.

Kariuki had hoped that a good night's sleep would resolve the impasse. He was to be disappointed. It remained with him through breakfast, at his office and into the next evening leaving him no option but to go for broke in his quest to unravel the conundrum.

'Moses,' he told his faithful bloodhound, 'I have another job for you.'

* * *

'Solomon,' said Moses, 'I have another job for you.'

Solomon could hardly believe his luck. With things going from bad to worse at the garage, anything that might help pay the bills was welcome. But this was beyond his wildest imaginings. Moses was offering to pay for a grand safari right across Kenya, if that's what it took, just to keep tabs on a man whose mode of transport you could almost see from space. There was hardly anyone in Kenya who didn't know the Millennium Falcon.

'Your job,' said Moses, 'is to go anywhere Kearney goes and report back on everything he does, especially if he stops to hack at rocks or scoop anything up from the ground. If he does, get a piece of anything he's collecting and bring it back.

'But make sure he doesn't see you. If he does, he'll know someone's on to his little game and will do anything – ANYTHING – to prevent that someone getting back with news of his find. His determination to keep the source of the "Blood of Christ", as the pastor puts it, secret will know no bounds.'

Moses was impressed with the pastor's euphemism even if it was intended to fool him into thinking he was doing the work of The Great Creator, not that of someone with more earthly interests. As soon as Kariuki had described the target of Kearney's explorations Moses knew precisely what he was after. Something that was very much of this world, not the one to which his pastor was alluding.

'Kearney the blasphemer has been sent by the Devil to locate the one thing he needs to overthrow the House of God and consign the whole of humanity to the fiery furnace,' Kariuki had fulminated at Moses.

'God has come to me in a vision and beseeched me and all members of this church not to rest until he is stopped. So be under no illusion Moses. As my right hand man in this endeavour, be assured that this is the most important responsibility you will ever undertake. The future of God's world depends on you. Prevent Kearney delivering the Blood of Christ to the Devil and unconditional deliverance will be yours for eternity.'

As Moses stood stock still before the pastor, jaw hanging open, gradually the enormity of what he was being asked to do dawned on him. Fully so when Kariuki set out in detail what it was Kearney should be prevented from delivering to the Devil.

'God has told me that the Blood of Christ takes many forms in this mortal world,' said Kariuki, 'three of which are secreted in the rocks of Kenya.

'The first is a liquid which oozes red from the rock to signify Christ's torment on the cross. The second is a crystalline form of the first, God's way of telling us that if we repent, all our sins will be forgiven. The third is in the form of a red powder, a reminder of what we will become of us lest we repent.

'Your mission, Moses, is to act as the eyes and ears of both God and this church. Should the man Kearney locate the substance in any of the above forms, you are to wait until he leaves, collect a sample of whatever it is he has located and deliver it to me personally so that those with the power to exorcise the Devil in him can fulfil God's work. Do nothing to prevent him in his mission. That will just anger the Devil into taking possession of more like Kearney to do his evil work. Understand?'

Too right, I understand, thought Moses. You're using me to get your hands on a bit of red mercury.

Moses might have been pious but he wasn't stupid. He knew the description of the mythical substance as well as anyone and his pastor had just described three of the forms it was reputed to take. You could read about it in any newspaper when the paper was short of real news to report.

Even so, Moses held his peace. He had no wish to antagonise his pastor who, after all, was surely only doing what he'd been told to do. Kariuki's higher power had obviously told him to describe the substance in a manner that every ardent follower of Christ could comprehend. They might struggle with the more scientific version.

Moses wondered which version he should present to Solomon since it wouldn't be Moses who'd be doing the tailing. In the end he decided to give it to Solomon straight. Although his cousin wasn't the shiniest spanner in the box, Moses had more respect for Solomon's intelligence than the pastor clearly had for his.

It wasn't that Moses was offended as such. More that he now had a better idea of the real level of esteem in which his pastor held him. To the pastor he was the equivalent of St Peter, the rock on which the church was built. But still a rock. One who probably needed to be spared the finer details of the church's grand designs.

Designs like Kariuki's reasons for going after the source of red mercury. That was what the pastor was doing, Moses was sure of it. But why? What interest could the church possibly have in a substance that was mythical at best, whose only reported use was as an enhancing agent in tactical nuclear weapons and which Kenya was under orders from its western allies to stop falling into the hands of potential enemies. The only value it had was in what those enemies would give for it.

'Oh dear God,' thought Moses. 'Surely not. Surely that's not the pastor's intention.'

But the more Moses thought about it, the more stubbornly the possibility stuck. Could his pastor really be thinking of selling Kenya's allies out? That really would be doing the Devil's work. Every one of the West's enemies was a godless blasphemer and denier of the one true faith. Moses knew it from his work at the Chinese News Agency. Could Kariuki really be contemplating doing business with the likes of them?

No, Moses told himself. That can't be it. There HAS to be another reason. The pastor is a devout Christian, a patriot and a pillar of the establishment. But Kearney isn't. Maybe it's him who's intending to do business with the West's enemies and Kariuki's out to stop him.

But if that's the case, why involve me? Surely he should be getting the security services to tail the Irishman.

'Oh dear God…'

chapter twenty-seven

Everyone seemed to be going on safari. Except Moses.

Kearney was clearly gearing up for one. The Chinese were in the process of preparing their own expedition. And Solomon was putting the money Kariuki had given Moses to good use restoring to safari condition an old, dysfunctional Landcruiser cluttering up his garage.

Only Moses looked like being left behind, news that had come just a week after being told he'd be acting as the Chinese expedition's driver/navigator.

Why, he'd wondered? Had he done something wrong or was there a connection between the Xinhua chief administrator's change of heart and a chance meeting between Kearney and the Chinese security man who accompanied Moses on every expedition equipment purchasing trip?

At first Moses wasn't upset he wasn't going. He hardly relished the idea of an extended trip into the wilderness with people he had trouble communicating with and who'd ensure all his worldly needs went unfulfilled for the duration.

But the more he thought about it, the more troubled he became.

There was every possibility that the chief administrator's mind change not only had nothing to do with the piece of paper Kearney had slipped Moses' Chinese minder but signalled something that for Moses could be *matata kubwa*, big trouble.

Could this be the beginning of the end of his employment at Xinhua? Was he being told, in a backhanded sort of way, that he was now surplus to the administrator's requirements… in more ways than one?

If he was, Moses knew there'd be little he could do to get her to change her mind except go into begging mode. Yes, he'd have to plead, he knew he was no young buck possessed of the boundless energy she demanded of her sexual partners but surely she could see he still had a few good gallops in him. Wasn't there something he could do to make her think again?

Moses knew it'd be a fruitless task. The administrator's heart was as cold as her animalistic antics between the sheets. Like a black widow spider she knew what she wanted, took it without asking, consumed both it and her victim in full and left nothing behind to link her to the crime. If she acted any differently when it came to the hiring and firing of people in her employ it'd be most out of character.

All of which, in the cold light of day, left Moses quaking. He could see the time coming when any employment, well-paid or otherwise, would be beyond finding.

Which would leave him with *matata kubwa* indeed. With no western-style social security safety net, Kenya and just about every other country in Africa expected the old and worn-out to be cared for by their offspring. Without such support, unless you both possessed and could still work on your *shamba*, you simply starved. That was the way of it and the result was an African population explosion to rival the locust swarms that rampaged across the continent leaving nothing but devastation in their wake.

Just like every other African of Moses' age, he'd done his bit to add to Africa's population bomb primarily to avoid being left abandoned, alone and uncared-for in his dotage… pretty much the only forward planning he, and every other African he knew, had ever done.

But now he was being forced to face up to the reality of having no contingency plan. His five children were still not of an age to support him and his brothers and sisters were even more resource poor than himself. If he wasn't earning, he realised, there'd be no alternative but to join the ranks of the thousands forced to live in the twilight zone on the edge of legitimate society.

It was not a prospect that generated great hope and joy in the God-fearing Moses' heart. Although he'd flirted with less-than legal activity in the past, that was before he found Jesus. And now he knew that admission through the pearly gates was restricted to the truly repentant and pure of heart he'd vowed never to tread the path of unrighteousness ever again.

That vow was now looking seriously under threat. How could he possibly keep it when every path for keeping body and soul together led to the breaking of the eighth commandment? A life of petty pilfering and jail dodging would be unavoidable unless some kindly employer took pity on him or he was somehow able to amass a legitimate bankroll to see him through until the Lord called his name.

With kindly employers and legitimate bankrolls almost as much of an endangered species as Moses himself, all looked lost. The only thing sustaining him was faith. Faith that the God he'd devoted the most recent years of his life to would not desert him in his hour of need.

* * *

When it came, it came in much the same way Moses had read St Paul's enlightenment on the road to Damascus had come. Out of nowhere, the answer presented to him was so blindingly obvious it had Moses beating his temples for not having thought of it himself.

'Thank you, thank you Lord,' he whimpered, sinking to his knees in supplication. 'I KNEW you wouldn't let me down.'

Moses immediately set off in search of Solomon. Only a fellow believer would accept without question that the flash of inspiration could only have been implanted in Moses' brain by the one true God.

Solomon gawped as Moses laid out his plan of action, not least because its whole basis centred on questioning the motives of the man who'd showed them both the path to redemption and eternal bliss.

Moses could see he'd have his work cut out convincing his cousin.

'I know it sounds like blasphemy but God himself told me. God has revealed Pastor Kariuki to be a false prophet. The man is using us to enrich himself. That's why he's got us tailing the Irishman. Kearney has something the pastor wants. Something he plans to profit from by doing a deal with the Devil incarnate.

'Believe me, Solomon, God is angry. He wants the pastor stopped and has placed responsibility for stopping him in the hands of you and me. How can we deny such a call? THAT would be blasphemy.'

'But the PASTOR! You cannot be serious,' gasped Solomon. 'Apart from Jesus, never has a man with such a godly mission ever walked the Earth.'

'Will you deny the word of God? Will you pass by on the other side when He calls your name?'

Solomon knew he was trapped. Doing what Moses was all but accusing him of doing would be to forsake the very premise on which the church he belonged to was founded. And when Moses laid out his reasons for suspecting Kariuki's motives, Solomon found himself being sucked irredeemably in.

His pastor, Solomon now saw, was clearly a charlatan. God had said so and had shown Moses the true path to redemption. One that would not only nip the evil one's intentions in the bud but see both Moses and himself richly rewarded for their pains – on Earth as it is in heaven, Solomon couldn't help murmuring to himself.

*   *   *

After his 'talk' with God, Moses realised where the inspiration for his plan to expose and unseat Kariuki had sprung from. It went right back to that moment when he'd been unable to contain his excitement about being given responsibility for shopping for the Xinhua 'film' crew's equipment and, in direct contravention of the warning he'd been given by his employer, had blabbed about it to the pastor.

Moses had always wondered why a light had come on in the pastor's eyes when Moses told him. Especially when he'd mentioned who the Chinese were using to organise their safari.

On previous occasions when Moses had cornered Kariuki with news to impart, the most he'd ever got was a polite smile and a few seconds of the pastor's time. This time, Kariuki not only stopped what he was doing but listened intently as Moses' story unfolded.

Now Moses knew why. The pastor had caught a glimpse of gold in the news his parishioner was bringing him. Red gold in this case.

Kariuki's ulterior motive hadn't presented itself to Moses straight away. It'd taken a few twists and turns for that to happen, starting with being asked, out of the blue, to tail Kearney around Nairobi. Moses had thought it an odd request but so fired up was he with being given this new responsibility that it went largely unquestioned. His pastor had his reasons and that was good enough for the pastor's parishioner.

But then had come the 'Blood of Christ' moment after Moses had reported Solomon's sighting of the government document in

Kearney's possession and suddenly, for the first time, Moses' brow wrinkled.

It was the pastor's unwillingness to use the substance's real name that had planted the seed of doubt in Moses' mind… and, the more Moses thought about it, of insult. Kariuki had clearly wanted to hide what he was really after and considered Moses so God-besotted and bible punch drunk that he'd accept the 'Blood of Christ' description without question.

Up to that moment, Moses had never had cause to doubt the word and teachings of the one who, until now, had had Moses convinced he'd received a personal visit from the Almighty. Now, for the first time, Moses found himself wondering if even that was a lie and whether there was anything more than just an arm up his pastor's sleeve.

To begin with he brushed it off, telling himself he obviously hadn't conveyed his true level of intelligence to his pastor. That he'd done nothing to dissuade his mentor from the assumption that he was no less vacuous than the average redemption-seeking church-goer. Hence the pastor's use of religious symbolism to convey his red mercury hunting requirements.

But hard as he tried to quell it, the feeling of disappointment that had consumed him over being treated like one of Kariuki's more simple-minded worshippers had not only not left him, it had, like an untreated wound, festered.

The day Moses heard he was being pulled off the Chinese expedition had been the day the wound turned septic. From feeling a valued member of society, Moses suddenly felt cast out. First he'd found his pastor didn't respect him and now he'd been effectively consigned to the rubbish bin by his employer. Why? Was it all his fault or was there more to this than met the eye? It was enough to drive a man to drink and Moses thought it churlish to deny the call.

Three bottles of White Cap later and Moses had the enlightenment he sought. The common denominator in all this had to be the 'Blood of Christ', he was sure of it, and as the contents of the bottles began to take effect, the jumble in Moses' head started sorting itself out.

Kearney had a map with the word 'red' written on it, Kariuki had commanded him to tail Kearney on any expedition out of town, and now he'd seen the Irishman surreptitiously passing a note to Moses' Chinese minder. What it said, Moses knew not. But he'd almost put money on it being something to do with red mercury.

From what he now knew, it seemed inconceivable that Kearney didn't have a shrewd idea where the fabled substance was. If he was Kearney, what would he do with the knowledge? He'd be off on a hunt for it with the aim of selling what he found to the highest bidder. The Chinese? It looked very much like it.

But how did Kariuki fit into all this? All the evidence pointed to the pastor coming to the same conclusion as Moses about the contents of the map. That's why he'd ordered Moses to follow Kearney into the bush. He was using Kearney and Moses to do all the hard graft with the intention of pouncing if it looked like he'd found something of interest.

But how would he pounce? Unless Kariuki had a secret army Moses knew nothing about he'd never get anything off the Irish gorilla and his Neanderthal sidekick without coming off second best.

So no, ambush was probably out. But not, it suddenly dawned on Moses, pouncing on the source once Kearney had left. That's why Kariuki wanted Moses to collect any samples of the 'Blood of Christ' Kearney found. Of course! That's what Kariuki was doing. Once Kearney had found it, Kariuki could simply swan in and fill his pockets with the stuff.

But then what? The only way Kariuki was going to profit from it was to sell it on. But to who? It seemed unlikely he'd be able to do a deal with the Kenyan government or its western allies. The map was on government headed paper meaning they already knew the source. And anyway, Moses was pretty sure that anyone trying to sell what must be a classified secret back to its owner would find himself becoming a classified secret soon after.

So no, Moses told himself. Kariuki wouldn't risk that. Which left only one other option. One Moses scarcely dared factor into the equation.

His pastor, the man who'd convinced the multitude that he'd talked to God, the man who'd convinced everyone he was doing God's work, was intending to put a material whose only use was to destroy the world God had made into the hands of a blaspheming infidel denier of all things holy and all in the name of profit.

'Oh dear God,' Moses wailed to himself. 'The bastard! Kariuki's planning to get a sample of the substance back to Nairobi before Kearney in order to make Kearney's deal with the Chinese redundant.'

Like Jesus, Moses wept.

* * *

By the end of Moses' reasoning, Solomon was weeping too.

'The utter, utter.… shit.' There was only one word for Kariuki. One that was only available in English and one Solomon hadn't used since becoming a follower of Kariuki's church. Now, he was prepared to make an exception.

'Shitshitshitshitshit! You're right Moses. The evil shit has to be stopped. Please tell me you have a plan.'

Moses smiled for the first time since bringing news of his conversation with God to his cousin.

'I think so. But it's not my plan. God is channelling His holy will through us. He has shown me the way and has told me what must be done.

'But He has also warned that it is not without risk. The road is rocky and long and we should be prepared for danger along the way. But accomplish this task, He has said, and we can be assured of receiving His eternal gratitude, both on Earth and in the hereafter.'

By the time Moses had finished outlining the means God had shown him for bringing Kariuki to heavenly justice, Solomon too was smiling.

God, he'd decided, was not only great but more than a little devious. The plan he'd planted in Moses' head would kill not just two but three birds with one stone. It'd make sure Kariuki received his just desserts, it would save the world He had created and, into the bargain, would solve the more Earthly problems of both him and his cousin.

chapter twenty-eight

'**D**' yous tink yous should be wearin' a tie?'

'Yeah, probably. You got one?'

Ryan just looked at his countryman. Even if he did own a tie, as Kearney knew full well it'd be in his toolbox, an emergency replacement for a broken fan belt.

Kearney had an appointment. One he was sure was going to change their fortunes for ever. The day before he'd received a phone call he'd interpreted as an invite to the embassy. It was difficult to tell. The Chinese accent made deciphering the message a matter of informed guesswork.

Kearney hoped to hell he'd guessed right. If it wasn't the Chinese embassy there'd not only be an awkward moment or two on his arrival but he'd be missing a meeting that could see him and Ryan home free with the pot of gold that'd remained just out of their reach for over a quarter of a century.

'Ach', said Kearney, 'it HAS to be the embassy. Your man's directions said Kilimani. That's where the embassy is.'

Ryan just looked at Kearney again. From what Kearney had told him about how the invitation had come about, it was lucky he'd had any response at all to his initial approach, let alone one from what might or might not be the embassy. The scribbled note Kearney had planted on the man he'd recognised from the Turkana expedition almost made it sound like they were planning to blackmail the people behind the safari.

'Is dat de best a man o' letters loike yousself could do?' sneered

231

Ryan when Kearney related his chance meeting with the man and Moses in the only safari supplies store that had yet to cancel Kearney's credit.

'I wasn't prepared,' mumbled Kearney. 'I never expected to see THEM in there. But when they walked through the door I had to take the chance. With Moses refusing to tell us who they were and how to contact them, I had no other option.'

'Yous coulda followed dem.'

'No petrol.'

'Eejit.'

Ryan's opinion of his friend hardly improved when Kearney outlined the contents of the note scrawled on the scrap of paper he'd blagged from the storekeeper.

'Hello,' he'd written, 'we know what you want. Our discretion and a shortcut to finding it are both available at very reasonable terms via the phone number below. All the best, A. Kearney.'

'Our feckin' discretion?' scoffed Ryan. 'All the feckin' best? Who d'yous tink yous blackmailin'? Yous feckin' auntie?'

'Like I said, I didn't have much time. Anyway, it seems to have worked. The note seems to have ended up in the right hands. Wasn't expecting the embassy though. The blokes I took on safari didn't look like diplomats to me.'

* * *

Neither, as it turned out, did the diplomats. More like teashop owners, thought Kearney as he stepped smiling from the Chinese embassy later in the day, a verbal contract in his pocket.

'Just goes to show how appearances can deceive,' he thought, thinking through the deal he'd just cut with four of the most nondescript men he'd ever seen.

In a meeting that had lasted all of ten minutes, Kearney had been ushered into an almost bare room, had been joined there by four virtually identical embassy officials who'd declined to identify themselves, had been invited to expand on his note and had then had to wait a moment while the men conferred outside.

'Proof,' said one of the men re-entering the room.

Kearney was ready for him. In his pocket was a copy of the map's letterhead and title – 'Geological Formations Concurrent With Red Mercury Manifestation' – with the map itself blanked out.

More conferring then 'Price?'

Kearney was ready for that one too. Also for the looks of bemusement on four almost identical faces when he outlined his terms.

'Solar?'

'Yes. Lots of it.'

'No money?'

'No. Just the solar panels… and air compressors.'

'How?'

It took Kearney just minutes to fill in the blanks. They'd get a regular drip feed of locations from the map, he told them, in return for regular supplies of the parts he wanted… at no cost to himself.

More conferring then 'We interest. Must consider more. We call.' And with that they were gone leaving Kearney in the company of the muscleman Kearney had slipped the note to.

Kearney tried to gauge something from his minder's face as he was escorted out of the building. Nothing. The man's expression remained as featureless as the block-built edifice he was being escorted out of.

'No matter,' grinned Kearney to himself. 'I think you could say that the seed is well and truly sown.'

Kearney and Ryan expected a couple of sleepless nights after that. Partly because they thought it'd take at least that long for the

Chinese to make a decision. Partly because they'd already started celebrating.

So when the phone call came early the next day, they were about as prepared for it as their homeland was for drought.

'Come embassy. We talk,' said the Chinese voice to the bottle of whisky in Kearney's brain. 'Ask Mr Wu.'

'Shit.'

'Wassat?'

'Fockin' Chinese. Wanna talk,' croaked Kearney to Ryan.

'Al-feckin'-ready?'

'Seems they're ready to blow up the world but can't do it without us.'

'Well dey can feckin' wait. Oi ain't goin' ter meet moi maker without a full Oirish inside me 'n dat's a fact.'

Two vast cholesterol-defying Irish breakfasts later and the pair were ready. Kearney for his meeting with the Chinese, Ryan for a nervous wait outside the embassy with the engine running in case they needed to make a quick getaway.

Half an hour later with the engine glowing white hot and Ryan beginning to wonder if he'd ever see his countryman again, Kearney finally emerged.

'Go! Go!' shrieked Kearney to a wide-eyed Ryan. 'Get going before the fockers change their minds!'

Careering away up the Ngong Road in a cloud of burning oil fumes the pair were well past the rugby club before Kearney stopped glancing behind him and breathed out.

'OK, you can slow down now. If they were thinking of following us we'd have seen 'em by now.'

'Followin' us? Dat must've gone well den,' said Ryan.

'Actually it did. But it always pays to be careful. Like the Arabs say, "trust in God…"'

'"… but tether yous camel",' chimed-in Ryan finishing off the

234

saying Kearney always resorted to when trying to encourage Ryan to look before leaping. 'Yeah, yeah. Yous can talk.'

'I resemble that remark,' countered Kearney, quoting one of Ryan's oft-used Malapropisms back to him. 'My planning was meticulous on this occasion. If it hadn't been, d'you think you'd now be looking at the man who's got a deal to beat all deals?'

'On paper, is it?'

'Not yet. But one more meeting should do it. They've sent me away to map out exactly how the arrangement would work.'

'Feck. Just don't be puttin' moi name on it.'

'Wasn't intending to. Mine neither. Just the raw details of what they get in return for what I want and a rough idea of how the transaction would take place. Shouldn't take too much effort.'

Two days later and Kearney was rueing ever having been so complacent. Having never had to map such a document out before he was beginning to understand why lawyers charged so much.

'Fock, this is complicated,' he whined at Ryan. 'Whenever I think I've got all the angles covered, another bloody pothole appears.'

Ryan just grinned. There were definite advantages to being semi-literate.

By the end of the second day, Kearney reckoned he had it. Strewn around him lay the product of hours of trying to get the wording right and in his hand something that, to him at least, didn't look like the contractual equivalent of Swiss cheese.

In the first instance, he'd written, in return for receiving directions to four of the locations on the map, the Chinese were to provide him with a 'receipt' for 'payment' for four solar/air compressor systems as detailed in the system's specifications Kearney had drawn up, the locations only to be revealed to the Chinese once the systems had cleared customs at Mombasa and been inspected by Kearney to his full satisfaction.

After that, the number of systems required for providing each additional red mercury location would rise exponentially by a factor of ten.

If, in the event of the Chinese deciding they needed no further locations before Kearney had unveiled the entire list, a compensation clause would be invoked requiring the Chinese to provide a 'receipt' for 'payment' for five hundred of the systems, cleared through the port and inspected to Kearney's full satisfaction before the contract was deemed expired.

'I think that covers everything,' Kearney said, slumping back in his chair. 'If it doesn't then we only have ourselves to blame.'

'We?'

'Yes Ryan, we. This bit of paper's going nowhere until you yourself have checked it. For once in my life I'm not going to rely on my own judgement alone. And since you're the only other person in this room, I'd say that makes you document-checker-in-chief.'

'Feck.'

To Kearney's amazement, not only did Ryan suggest a re-wording of a couple of un-watertight phrases but even found the odd spelling mistake.

'Dat's not how yous spell "receipt", yous feckin' eejit. Where'd yous go ter school? Somewhere dat obviously don't teach der 'i' before der 'e' ting by der looks of it. Udderwise, not too bad.'

More amazingly still, that's also what the Chinese thought. Within minutes of seeing Kearney's proposal they looked at one another, then at Kearney and nodded.

'Shit,' thought Kearney. 'Should've made it a factor of twenty.'

* * *

Kearney and Ryan's excitement grew as they waited for the call confirming the components they wanted had arrived at Mombasa and were being cleared by the Chinese to await Kearney's inspection.

Was this it? Had they finally cracked the code that'd lead to that cherished escape from their African Guantanamo? It was beginning to look like it. Surely nothing could go wrong now and the pair began to celebrate... much to the amusement of a certain sinister presence looking on with a sly, malevolent smirk on his face. In their rapture the pair had forgotten about Mwangi, his law and the unlimited supply of spanners at his disposal.

With such a deliciously hope-wrecking target presenting itself how could Mwangi resist? Here was a dream so ripe for destruction it had him salivating at the prospect and Mwangi knew precisely which of his spanners would wreak the most havoc in the Kearney/Ryan firmament. A simple whisper in the ear of two hitherto unrelated parties should do it, both intent on cashing in at Kearney's expense before the man had any inkling that the rug was moving beneath his poorly-shod feet.

So while Kearney and Ryan drank toasts to their impending coup, Mwangi was getting busy. While the Chinese were having a revelation over the means of relieving Kearney of his solar power venture for their own nefarious ends Kariuki was punching the air over the flash of inspiration that had arrived for making whatever deal Kearney had with the Chinese obsolete.

'Think about it,' hissed Mwangi in Kariuki's ear. 'All you have to do is fit the Irishman with a tail. That'll lead you to where X marks the spot and Kearney will be none the wiser when you descend later to gather up enough material to interest the buyer of your choice. Why not the Chinese? That's where Kearney's journey seems to have begun.'

And ended reasoned Moses after receiving Solomon's reports of the Irishman showing no sign of leaving town. The only place Kearney had gone, his cousin had told him, was to the Chinese embassy, three times. Then he'd effectively gone to ground, only emerging from his bunker on the odd drinking expedition.

Moses' brow had wrinkled at the news. Surely Kearney would be anxious to get on the road. It looked like he was gearing up for a trip when their paths had crossed on Moses' safari shopping expedition. But here he was two weeks later still in town and not looking like going anywhere. It didn't make sense.

Neither did it make for worthwhile reports to Kariuki.

'No, pastor,' Moses kept having to inform him. 'He still in Nairobi,' conveniently forgetting to add in the bit about where in Nairobi. The last thing he wanted was for Kariuki to begin suspecting that Moses was suspecting there was more to this than a search for the 'Blood of Christ'. If Kariuki knew he knew there was a Chinese connection he might very well start getting the jitters and stop paying Moses to keep an eye on Kearney.

So no, Kearney's visits to the embassy would not be mentioned. But that still left Moses wondering what the Irishman was doing in there and why he showed no sign of going anywhere else.

'What would you do in Kearney's position?' he wondered out loud to Solomon. 'You've got the map. You've got a buyer for the product. What would stop you going and getting it?'

'Maybe the small print. Maybe they're still having palaver about the detail.'

'Could be. If you were the *mzungu*, what deal would suit you best? What'd be the best way of making the most of what you knew?'

'Setting up a regular supply agreement?'

'Maybe. But how could you be certain the Chinese weren't tailing you when you went to collect more? Unless you were very devious, you'd risk leading them to the source. And once the location secret is blown, that would be that. No more red mercury business.'

'You could lay a false trail. Lead the Chinese somewhere else while someone else goes to the real place.'

'You could. But that'd probably only work once. The Chinese have probably got all sorts of tracking devices they'd use after realising they'd been duped.'

Moses and Solomon looked into their bottles of White Cap searching for inspiration.

It was Solomon who finally broke the silence.

'Maybe Kearney's not looking for a regular supply deal at all. Maybe he's more interested in a one-off, charging a big lot for what he's got and for information as to where they could go for more.'

'Could be,' mumbled Moses. 'That'd also definitely be the less risky way of doing it. Going regularly would be dangerous. They'd probably throw away the key if they found any on you.'

Silence again, then a flash of inspiration.

'Or, he could just be selling the map! That would explain two things. Why he's been going to the embassy so often, why he's still in Nairobi and why the Chinese have decided to go on their "filming" expedition without me! They're not bloody filming at all! They're bloody mining.'

chapter twenty-nine

Xi Ren was truly glad to be going back on the road. After two false starts and over a month back in the Xinhua prison, he was beginning to experience something he hadn't experienced since first finding himself confined to a Xinhua editing cubicle.

Although this time he had something more than the mindless Xinhua work to occupy him, the claustrophobia was still a trial and the chief administrator's irritating mind changes weren't helping.

First, Xi was told they'd only be back from the field a few days while their new safari guide Moses was gathering supplies for the next stage of the 'filming' operation. Then a delay when the administrator realised that the news agency's four-wheel drive allocated to them needed to be made Xinhua-identification free. Then another when she decided that this was to be a Xinhua-only operation and that the security man replacing Moses needed to be fully Kenya geography re-educated.

While that mind-numbing process was underway, Xi kicked his heels in the compound going over the safari route map time and again until he could see it with his eyes closed.

And his escape routes. This, he'd decided, was to be his last confinement inside the Xinhua prison walls. He'd seen what lay beyond and liked what he saw – miles and miles of wilderness and places they'd never think of looking for him.

First, though, he had to suffer just a couple more days of penal servitude. The administrator was clearly in discussion with someone about their forthcoming trip and wasn't about to order its commencement until sure all was in place.

Then, finally, they were off and to Xi's astonishment headed away from what he'd suggested should be their first destination. Not back to Baringo to pick up where they'd left off, but west towards Lake Victoria.

What had inspired this plan change without consulting him Xi knew not and didn't care to ask. Despite having been put *de facto* in charge of the hunt for red mercury, he knew when not to open his mouth – and that the change of plan had to be linked to whatever advice she'd been receiving from person or persons unknown.

Sitting in the back of the Xinhua vehicle as it wove between Nairobi's limitless supply of potholes out towards the marginally better-kept road to Kisumu, with no one else to turn to for an explanation of the change of plan Xi found himself debating the issue with himself.

She was clearly under pressure to revise it. That much was clear. But that didn't explain everything. Could it have something to do with her being relatively new to the administrator job? Was she still feeling her way? Being super-cautious to ensure all the bases were covered with nothing being overlooked?

Yes, Xi told himself. That was probably it. It was all about caution bred from inexperience. And now he came to think about it, that inexperience could also explain something else that had left him scratching his head.

'Salary?' Xi had almost said out loud when the administrator had almost offhandedly told him that, despite his new responsibilities, it wasn't going to change.

'The woman must be confusing me with one of the regular members of staff,' he'd thought at the time. 'She knows as well as I do that no one saddled with a debt to pay to society receives

242

anything to pay it with. All they get is four walls, a bed, an interminable workload and grit-filled rice for breakfast, lunch and dinner.'

With everything else on his mind, not least his escape plan, Xi hadn't dwelt on what he'd assumed to be an honest mistake. But now they were on the road and he had nothing else to do except stare at the passing bush out of the vehicle's window, he found the word returning to him and demanding further attention.

It was a strange one. Could she really have been so preoccupied with the expedition planning she'd forgotten who she was talking to?

Yeah, surely. How could it be anything other?

'Really?' Xi found his inner voice intervening. 'Sure about that? Do you seriously believe she'd allow herself to overlook the fact that she was in conversation with a convicted felon over something that could make or break her career?'

'But what else could it be? She knows I don't get a salary.'

'Does she?'

'Sorry?'

'Think about it. She is quite new. Could it be that she really is under the impression that you're a regular member of staff?'

'How could that be? She has my file.'

'Precisely.'

'Sorry? Not sure…'

'Have a little think about it.'

Xi's eyes widened as he did.

'No. You can't seriously be suggesting…'

Silence.

'Oh come on! Surely not.'

Nothing.

'Oh shit. You are serious. You mean…'

'… that you really are a regular member of staff? Yes. And

before you go poo-pooing the idea let me ask you this. Have you ever really thought about what transpired at that final meeting with the editor in Beijing? What was it he asked you to sign?'

'A contract.'

'Why?'

'What d'you mean "why?"'

'Why would there be any need? You're an enemy of the state. A damned subversive and a felon. The editor could have packed you off with a snap of his fingers. He had the power to do with you as he pleased!'

'Holy fuck,' Xi almost said out loud as they approached Kisumu. 'You're right. If he needed my agreement to be posted here, that means he had no real hold over me.'

'And what does that mean?'

Silence.

'It means, you dull-witted dim sum, that your sentence had expired sometime before you were sent here and that "someone" neglected to mention it.

'Not only that but that you officially had a salary! Wonder what happened to that then?'

* * *

Watching the Xinhua expedition pull out, the only things going through Moses' mind were 'good riddance', 'hope you get lost' and 'may you find yourselves bogged up to your axles in a snake-infested swamp'. Good Samaritan sentiments didn't apply to godless heathen. And anyway, after finding out what the pastor was up to, he was beginning to wonder how much longer he could count himself one of his church's flock. Not long, he suspected, once Kariuki discovered the truth behind the present Moses was planning to give him.

244

For his patience in keeping Moses, and by association Solomon, on the all-expenses- paid Kearney-watching job for a full four weeks, Moses thought Kariuki deserved a reward. But he couldn't give it him while Kearney remained in Nairobi. If the two ran into one another, it'd put paid to the story Moses had cooked up to go with it.

As the days went by with Kearney going nowhere, Moses began fretting that not only would he never get the chance to deliver the gift but that Kariuki might decide to abandon the whole operation altogether.

But then, one day Kearney was gone, Solomon on his tail, and Moses breathed again. He'd give Kearney a couple of days to make sure it wasn't just a long weekend away, then he'd pay Kariuki a visit.

'He's in Mombasa,' Solomon said in his call back to Moses. 'He's been in and out of the port a couple of times and seems to be checking paperwork with the customs guys and a couple of Chinese. I think they might be trying to clear a container.'

It was just the news Moses needed. Well aware of the port officials' reputation for making life difficult for people having no option but to use the place, Moses knew it could take days just finding the container. It was time to drop in on the false prophet and give him a taste of his own despicable medicine.

* * *

Like Xi, Kearney had also been in prison. Not literally, but that's the way it felt. Neither he nor Ryan could remember the last time they'd gone a whole month without making some sort of foray into the bush. But on this occasion they'd held their peace. Both knew this was the big one. The one that could change their lives forever. So just this once they'd vowed to bide their time, curb their natural inclinations and stay alert for the call.

That hadn't prevented them taking the odd drink, of course. That really would have been out of character. But again, for once in their lives, they'd always left before chucking out time much to the astonishment and annoyance of the bartenders and the bars' female clientele. Both were feeling the pinch as a result of the pair's newfound and wholly unexplained self-denial.

By the end of their incarceration Kearney and Ryan were not only climbing the walls but beginning to think the Chinese had done the dirty on them, maybe even getting their own copy of the map.

But then had come the call and the pair had sprung chaotically into action. Kearney to Mombasa to check on the shipment arriving from China, Ryan to prepare the site they'd chosen to host their solar system's first off-grid trial, Bushwacker Camp.

While these two were chasing the rainbow they knew would bring untold riches, Moses too was starting to dream of a life beyond penury. Only Kariuki could help him and only if he was prepared to pay the price Moses was going to demand. In his possession was something the 'pastor' wanted and, Moses was confident, would pay almost anything to get.

* * *

'Moses! Moses! Come in! Sit down. *Chai*? *Kahawa*? *Fanta*?'

'No thank you, pastor. I have to be back at work in a few minutes.'

'So… is it true? You managed to get what we're looking for?'

'Yes, *mzee*. The infidel Irishman led me right to it.'

'And you managed to get a sample?'

'Yes, *mzee*. I have it.'

'Where? Show me!' pleaded Kariuki.

'It is safe, *mzee*.'

'You haven't brought it?'

'No, *mzee*.'

Kariuki looked at his parishioner through narrowed, newly-appreciative eyes. Moses was about to do to him what he'd spent his whole life doing to others. Respect, he thought. Damn the man.

'I see. And when do you expect to be bringing it?'

'Sometime soon, *mzee*.'

'I see. Is there some way of encouraging you to be more specific?'

'Yes, *mzee*.'

'And what sort of encouragement would be appropriate, do you think?'

'Something small, *mzee*?'

'How small? Gecko-size? Bush rat? Jackal?'

'Mmmmmm…'

'Bigger?'

'Mmmmmm…'

'How big? Cheetah? Hyena? Lion?'

'Mmmmmm…'

'You are beginning to test my patience Moses. Name your animal.'

'Errrr… elephant, *mzee*? Much time and much danger getting 'Blood of Christ' and my family are hungry.'

Kariuki was impressed. Moses was doing exactly what he'd do if he was in Moses position – enter the negotiation at the top end and be prepared to haggle. Once you'd started, you could never go up, only down.

Even so, he wasn't about to make life easy for the man in possession of the thing Kariuki currently craved above all else. Kariuki's years of experience had taught him there were ways of negotiating the price down to a level that suited him more than his adversary, starting in this case with drawing on the good book to remind his devout follower of God's thoughts on the matter of avarice.

'That's quite a big animal, Moses. An animal with a big appetite and you know from your bible studies how greed angers the Almighty. In Timothy we learn that "money is the root of all evil" and in Luke Jesus tells us "to be on guard against every form of greed, for life is not in possessions".

'What every God-fearing person must always remember, Moses, is that "it is more blessed to give than to receive", Acts 20:35, and that it is "better the little that the righteous have than the wealth of many wicked", Psalm 37.'

'Thank you, pastor. The word of God is great. But does it not also say in Samuel that "the Lord sends poverty and wealth; he humbles and he exalts"?'

'You have read your bible well,' said Kariuki, secretly rueing having employed a proper teacher to run the church's bible classes. 'But there are many more passages condemning greed than there are of lauding it. And never forget that in the final analysis it all comes down to what Jesus is quoted as saying in Matthew 5:5 – "Blessed are the meek, for they will inherit the earth".'

'Including the mineral rights, *mzee*?'

Kariuki blanched. 'Shit,' he thought, 'where did that come from? Does the little bastard know more than he's letting on? If so, he's not as green as he's *sukuma wiki* looking. This is beginning to look like checkmate.'

The self-same conclusion was going through Moses' mind. It wasn't often the pastor was struck dumb. Kariuki was now in no doubt about how Moses felt about having his intelligence insulted. 'Blood of Christ' indeed!

Moses knew something else too. From the look on the pastor's face, he knew that that was that for this stage of the negotiation. Kariuki knew he was trapped and there'd be no budging Moses from his elephant demand. The only thing left to agree on was the size of the elephant.

* * *

By the time Moses left the church he had what he wanted. A baby elephant for the promised 'Blood of Christ' sample, its mother for the sample's grid coordinates and an arrangement for the exchange. The only thing left to do was call Solomon back to town, complete the exchange then disappear off the face of the earth Kariuki had told him he'd be inheriting.

Two days later and the pair had done just that leaving Kariuki with a small phial of red powder, a map reference and a wallet slimmed down by several thousand dollars.

The more Kariuki looked at the phial, the more he congratulated himself. That could have proved way more costly, he kept assuring himself. Thank God it was only the meek of the earth he'd had to negotiate with. If it'd been Kearney, he'd probably be a goodly whack more out of pocket. Maybe even a bull elephant or two.

So, all in all, he'd made the right choice sending Moses after the substance. The animal he was thinking of charging for its onward sale to the Chinese would make his elephant outlay look mouse-like by comparison.

While Moses had been out in the field dogging Kearney's movements, Kariuki had had time to think. First about the price he thought the Chinese would pay for the red mercury and its location, second about how to go about demanding it.

From his earlier encounters with the Chinese he knew one thing. The shits couldn't be trusted. So caution would be paramount. That and making sure the deal – and payment in full – was in the bag before parting with anything.

He had Moses to thank for giving him a way in. He'd use the animal size negotiating tool that'd proved so effective with his now ex-parishioner. It said everything and nothing at the same time and, once a figure had been applied to the value of the animal in question, Kariuki could be assured of securing an amount not incomparable with the loss he'd sustained over the titanium supply scam.

Yes, he thought. That should just about do it. A single adult elephant for the sample. The herd for the location. Then it'd just be about deciding the size of the herd.

But first he'd have to make contact, not something he especially relished since it'd mean having to revisit the very people he'd sworn never to have anything to do with ever again. With no contacts inside the embassy, he'd have to use the titanium scammers to set up a meeting and all without giving anything away about what it was he wanted to talk about.

It'd be like doing business with a jackal, thought Kariuki. Somehow he'd have to keep a smile on his face while guarding his private parts. A bit like Kenyan politics, Kariuki mused.

* * *

Kariuki wasn't the only one with politics on his mind. As much as it'd have surprised Kariuki to hear it, it was also the focus of Moses and Solomon's.

Back in their Luo tribal heartland of Kisumu the pair were being given a hero's welcome by the Orange Democratic Movement, the Luo political opponent of the ruling, Kikuyu-dominated, Jubilee Party. The stunt Moses and Solomon had pulled on the despised Kikuyu would not only go down in Luo history but propel them sharply up the ODM ranks.

It wasn't just that they'd managed to infiltrate the Kikuyu inner circle. They'd also gained the confidence of one of the tribe's grandees, given him the run-around and finally got him to part with some serious money, a proportion of which was now helping the ODM's campaign to oust Uhuru Kenyatta and his Kikuyu cronies from State House.

To the Luo, this was not only beautiful but poetic. Especially the part about how the pair had not only fleeced Kariuki but virtually destroyed him.

The thought that he could be so easily duped surprised Moses and Solomon. They'd expected him to be more cautious in his dealings with them. But maybe they hadn't given enough weight to the Kikuyu greed factor. Well known for taking without asking, the Kikuyu's acquisitiveness was legendary. Kenya's biggest tribe hadn't become so big for nothing.

So perhaps the pair shouldn't have been so surprised when greed got in the way of scientific analysis.

Their relief in finding it had and that they'd read Kariuki right was palpable. If they'd miscalculated, there was every chance of them becoming lion food and of Kariuki's 'Blood of Christ' search continuing without them.

As it was, they were back in the sanctuary of Luo-land, both their and the ODM's coffers had been nicely replenished and all were slapping the backs of all the others at the thought of Kariuki's hands freezing in mid-rub on the discovery that the grail now locked securely away in his safe wasn't quite as holy as its finder had made out.

chapter thirty

'**B**ASTARDS!'
Kariuki was not a happy man and neither was his sister-in-law. Their day had just been ruined by a call from the Chinese embassy. They wouldn't, as originally agreed, be completing the transaction.

Not only did they want their money back but from the tone in the caller's voice Kariuki had been left in no doubt that his name was being transferred from the embassy's Christmas card list to the one containing names of those condemned to live in interesting times.

'How the fucking hell did that happen?' Beatrice Kinyui was apoplectic. In the space of thirty seconds she'd just seen her share of the venture's profits shrink from the equivalent of a brand new Mercedes to that of the air in its tyres. 'I thought you'd fucking checked!'

Kariuki just looked at his hands, unable to speak. He'd been so sure. As Kinyui had so delicately put it, how the fuck HAD that happened?

Through the fog of impending ruin swirling in his head, Kariuki tried to focus. If he could just pinpoint where he'd gone wrong there might still be a chance of at least getting his name off the 'interesting times' list. With a supreme effort, he indicated to Kinyui to calm down and let him think. There had to be a weak link in all this. Where was it?

Was it in his original request to Moses to stay on Kearney's tail?

In Moses' reports back? In his policeman friend's reports on the KWS man? In his instructions to Moses regarding the hunt for the 'Blood of Christ'? Or could it be those shits from the Chinese company who'd demanded even more money for putting him in contact with someone of influence at the Chinese embassy. The permutations were endless. It could, thought Kariuki, even be the shits at the embassy themselves. Were THEY lying too? There was only one way to find out.

'Get a magnet off the fridge door,' he told Kinyui. 'There's only one way to settle this.'

Kinyui was back in seconds to find her brother-in-law emptying the contents of a small bottle on to a sheet of paper.

'Thank God I didn't let them have all of it. This'll show if they're trying to scam us.'

Very slowly, Kariuki brought the magnet in contact with the powder then equally slowly removed it, the magnet quavering in his trembling hands as he looked on through fear-filled eyes.

'Shit. They're not lying.'

'How can you tell?'

'Mercury wouldn't react,' he said showing Kinyui the magnet, now covered in flecks of red powder.

'So what is it then?'

'Iron oxide,' Kariuki said through the hands covering his face. 'Fucking rust.'

* * *

How? What? Why? The questions haunted Kariuki long into the night as he sat in his office gradually transferring the contents of a bottle of whisky from bottle to liver. The what and why were obvious. How, was the question. And, the more he thought about it, who.

Gradually he whittled away at the list of suspects until only two remained – Moses and bloody Kearney.

It wasn't the Chinese, he muttered to himself. He'd already ruled them out with the test on the powder. Neither was it likely to be the policeman. Apart from the fact that he hadn't been made privy to what Kariuki was looking for, Kariuki had too much on him to risk pulling this sort of caper. So that left only Moses and Kearney.

Moses he already knew about. He'd been just the delivery boy of the package, a proportion of which Kariuki had then onpassed to the Chinese in return for an initial payment and the promise of the monetary equivalent of a herd of elephants for the find's location. Once tests on the sample proved positive there'd be more than enough to bail the church out, get the bank regulators off his back and leave a substantial wad for 'eventualities'.

The more he thought about it, the more the finger of suspicion fell on Kearney. He was the wildcard in all this. It'd be just the sort of stunt he'd pull 'for the craic that's in it' as he'd heard other Irishmen put it.

But why? How could it profit him? Was this more about revenge than money? Could Kearney really still be harbouring a grudge over Kariuki's dismissal of him and his project at that World Bank meeting? Very possibly. The Irish were well-known for simmering over the coals of a fire neither side could remember how got lit. Just look at Ireland's North/South conflict.

The more the name Kearney remained in the frame, the more it consigned all others to the waste bin until, in the early hours of the morning, Kariuki banged an imaginary gavel on the table and pronounced his verdict.

'YES! It HAS to be Kearney. He and Moses are in cahoots. Moses wouldn't have the wit or the daring to try something like this on his own. He's just Kearney's trained monkey.'

And with that Kariuki passed out to dream a dream of catching the Irishman red-handed – literally – before waking with a start just before the dream got to the bit about parting with a great deal of money for something he hadn't tested. His subconscious wouldn't allow it.

What it would allow was the outline of a plan for bringing retribution down on the head of his nemesis and for recouping some of the ground lost to Kearney's infernal interference. If he could find the man and wring a confession out of him in the presence of the Chinese there was a chance of not only regaining his *guanxi* contact with them, as the Chinese put it, but maybe even getting some of his money back. It was a long shot but he had to give it a try.

* * *

While Kariuki seethed and plotted, over at the Chinese embassy Mr Wu was breathing a sigh of relief. Thank goodness he hadn't relied totally on the African banker. If he had, after tests on the substance had proved negative, his search for a material that would put the People's Republic of China on equal terms with its nuclear adversaries would still be stalled at square one.

While he hoped Kariuki's sample would negate the need to continue scouring the country for the substance's source, defence attaché Wu had had the foresight to refrain from ordering his search team back to base. They hadn't turned anything up yet, but, Wu reassured himself, it was still early days. Apart from that first expedition to Turkana, the team had only visited three of the sites on Kearney's list.

While they were on their way to the fourth, Wu's mind had turned to the most appropriate way of reminding anyone thinking of doing a Kariuki on the Chinese of the likely consequences.

A severe and very public financial flogging seemed fitting for a banker, thought Wu. In one, it would send out the two signals Wu wanted out in the open. First, that you messed with the Chinese at your peril. Second, that China was either close to obtaining or had already obtained the one thing the West desperately wanted China not to obtain.

Until recent months, although China would have liked to be able to add red mercury to its list of strategic finds, it hadn't been accorded priority treatment. A wary détente had existed between China and the West making it unnecessary to enter what the Americans somewhat vulgarly called a dick measuring contest over their respective nuclear arsenals.

But that was under previous, less volatile, US administrations. The erratic behaviour of the new occupant of the White House had changed everything. The new man, concluded the Beijing cadres, wasn't only trigger-happy, he was about as stable as a mercury detonator. Put one foot wrong and he was just as likely to press the button as he was to post an ill-considered rant on Twitter... or even of getting the two send buttons mixed up.

The only thing that might make him hesitate, thought the cadres, would be the knowledge that China now had to capability to give as good as it got. Hence the urgent all-points bulletin to China's embassies to acquire red mercury at any cost – or at least to be giving a credible impression that the substance was now within China's grasp. Either way it was a deterrent.

Following receipt of the message from his superiors, Wu did something he'd never admit to doing. Convinced the world was entering its most dangerous phase since the Cuban missile crisis, he prayed.

'If there is anyone up there,' he said silently to no one in particular, 'I'd be very grateful if you'd steer my people in the direction of the one thing that could prevent us blowing up the thing they say you created. Put it in our hands and you can be sure of the gratitude of some seven billion inhabitants of your alleged creation. Thank you. End of message.'

Wu hoped Kearney was praying too. If the fourth site turned out to be as unproductive as the first three, Wu knew his confidence in the Irishman would start to waver and he'd have to start thinking of a fitting admonishment for having tried it on.

Making the company that owned the Guinness consortium an offer it couldn't refuse, sacking all the Dublin brewery workers, moving it to somewhere like Cambodia and blaming it all on Kearney might do the trick.

If he was honest with himself, thought Wu, his confidence in Kearney was never sky high in the first place. Especially after the man had revealed the first four sites. They were about as far from one another as it was possible to get in Kenya and, in Wu's estimation, the seller of the information had been rather too ready to double his two sites for two solar systems negotiating start point when Wu had countered with six for six.

In fact, thought Wu, Kearney's first list of sites could even be a little Irish joke. He'd heard how the Irish had a problem taking things seriously. Could this be an example of outlandish Irish impishness? If it was, it could even be possible that Kearney was sending Wu's search team to the furthest four points of the compass – northwest, northeast, southwest and southeast – to deliberately put them off the scent. Join up the lines between them and you'd have a cross. As in X marks the spot, mused Wu. Or, in this case, sport.

Not known for his sense of humour, Wu ruminated long and hard over the possibility of this being a wild Irish goose chase. If it was, Kearney was about to find out how humourless he could be. If the fourth and last location in the southeast failed to produce anything, Wu resolved to start giving serious thought to his Guinness brewery relocation idea.

Unaware of the threat that loomed over the maker of his favourite tipple, Kearney was dreaming of just that. It was about this time of day that he always dreamed of it. Of being able to stride contentedly into an Atlantic-lashed pub on the Galway seafront to find Mick the barman smiling over several pints of the creamy-headed black stuff pulled in timely anticipation of the arrival of the first of his regulars.

Even if you couldn't actually see it, everyone in Ireland knew the point in the sun's inclination that signalled the moment for toasting its imminent disappearance below the horizon and Kearney was no exception. He longed for the day when he could actually do it again, sit with his sundowner pint and raise a glass to the thing that'd be toasting him back if only it wasn't raining.

Looking at the upturned hulk of the Millennium Falcon lying forlornly at the foot of the ravine, Kearney wondered if that day would ever come. He'd done everything he could to make it happen. This was his last throw of the dice. He had nothing left. If this didn't do it, he'd be destined to spend the rest of his days chasing his tail across what Hemmingway had so succinctly described as 'miles and miles of bloody Africa'.

Until this most recent mishap – the result of rewarding himself with a leisurely drive to Bushwacker's via the overland back route after checking the contents of the Chinese containers at Mombasa – Kearney was convinced he and Ryan were home and dry. Or even wet. It didn't matter.

And now? Shit. Did a busted tie rod end portend impending doom?

'Not a-fockin'-gain,' Kearney mumbled as the disappearing African sun glinted off his fake, Chinese-made, Ray-Bans. He'd had enough of doom.

And of that scheming little sod Mwangi. This was his doing,

Kearney was sure of it. This was just the sort of stunt he'd pull to remind anyone thinking of taking advantage of Africa that they did so at their peril.

'Well, you malicious bastard,' he told the lizard, surely Mwangi the malevolent made flesh and here to gloat over Kearney's predicament, 'I'm not beaten yet. Ryan'll be along anytime now. You'll see. He'll be coming into view just about... now.'

The lizard's head followed Kearney's gaze westwards. If Kearney could see anything, he had better eyesight than him.

'OK, OK. He's probably hung up getting the panels and compressors unloaded from the container. They should've arrived at the camp by now. Yes, that'll be it. He knows where his priorities lie. The sooner the first system is up and running the sooner we've got something to show potential customers. He knows that's number one on the list. Not running around after me. He knows I can look after myself. He's probably waiting till the last moment before setting off. He'll be here soon enough. You see.'

The lizard was impressed. All this confident posturing when he could see in Kearney's eyes his mind was on something else. Something like this being what you get when you lie to people.

'All right, all right. I fockin' admit it,' Kearney eventually responded to the lizard's interrogating eye. 'I DID make up those four locations. I HAD to. There were only five on the list. If I'd named them outright, we'd never have got anywhere close to getting the number of systems we need to get the scheme going. It was a matter of means to a very justifiable end. The way I see it, doing our bit to get the world to go solar at least counteracts in some small way the efforts of others to destroy it. So no, lizard, before you ask, my conscience is clear. End of. Got it?'

The lizard wasn't listening. His attention was elsewhere, fixed on a point to the east, his head raised and his whole body tensed for a rapid escape should there be the need.

Now wholly in tune with the wilderness around him, Kearney knew when not to ignore the warning signs exhibited by its inhabitants. Following the direction of the lizard's snout, he jumped to his feet and clamped his binoculars to his eyes.

Sure enough, he could just spot a cloud of dust in the distance. From what? Large animals? Ones with big teeth and a healthy appetite? Nah. Lions crept up on you. They didn't kick up dust.

Buffalo did though. Kearney hated buffalo. They were probably the only animal in the bush that not only hated humans but didn't give a shit about what they might be armed with. He'd been charged by enough in his time even though both he and they knew he posed no threat. They just did it for the sheer, malicious hell of it.

'Fock,' said Kearney. 'Hope they're not bloody buffalo. Even hiding in the Falcon wouldn't save me. What's the plan lizard?'

Again the lizard wasn't listening. His attention was now turned to the west.

'Jeez, you wait hours for a bus and then…'

Away in the west was another cloud of dust, about the same size and distance as the first.

'FOCK! Am I in the middle of two buffalo stampedes heading directly towards one another?'

If he was, Kearney knew he was dead meat. He couldn't hide, there was nothing to climb and he sure as hell couldn't outrun them. The only thing he could do was monitor their approach and hope the hundreds of snorting vindictive beasts the size of a small truck and with an IQ to match left enough gaps between them to dodge through. It was a forlorn hope and Kearney knew it. Maybe a better plan was to pray for deliverance.

As he swung the binoculars back and forth trying to keep abreast of the beasts' trajectory, he began to wonder if the mere consideration of praying was as good as doing it. It seemed it might be. There'd been a change in the respective clouds of dust.

'Wait a minute,' he informed the lizard. 'Those aren't buffalo. The clouds are too well defined. And they're coming in faster than boefs can run. Those are cars or I'm not Kilkenny from County Killarney. And they're not hanging about either.

'I told you so lizard, you doubting bastard,' said Kearney hopping from one foot to the other in joy, 'I'm fockin' saved.'

As Kearney watched in glee, the only thing he didn't get was why. Why two cars? And why was one of them coming in from the east. The one coming from the west was Ryan, he was sure of that. But who was in the other? Did he have another extrasensory perception partner he knew nothing about? Or was it the brigands that ruled these parts? Well, he'd know soon enough.

Gradually, as the two cars closed in he could just make them out and didn't recognise either. He knew the Bushwacker Camp vehicles and neither fitted the description. They were way too new. Had Ryan started spending their money already? He bloody hoped not. They hadn't made any yet.

But there, he was sure, was Ryan in the one coming in from the west. So who was in the one from the east? He couldn't quite make him out.

'Wait a sec,' thought Kearney. 'What's Ryan doing in the passenger seat? Has he gone and bought a left-hand drive? That'd be typical. It's difficult enough driving on Kenya's roads in the right-hand seat. In the left, you'd be taking your life in your hands every time you went to overtake. Not that you don't already.'

Swinging back to the other car, he could now see the car clearly enough to see it was a right-hand drive.

'Hmmm. I think that if there's a choice of rescue vehicles, reckon I'll take the right-hand drive one. Ryan'll kill me in the left-hand drive and I think I've had enough excitement for one day.'

'It ain't over yet,' said Mwangi through the lizard.

He was right. As the vehicles got closer, Kearney could see why

Ryan was in the left-hand seat. Someone else was driving. An African. And the other car was full of people who weren't either European or African. They were Chinese.

Judging by the cars' respective speeds, it looked to Kearney like he was standing on the exact spot where East would finally collide with West. 'How very appropriate,' he thought.

'Wait a minute,' he quavered as the realisation struck. 'Those are the Chinese I took on safari. The one next to the driver is the nice one who made coffee for me and let slip about the red mercury. They must be coming back from the site I gave them in the Shimba Hills and they don't look especially happy. Oops.'

Once again Kearney began to pray. This time that Ryan and his African driver got to him first. He didn't fancy having a stand-up shouting match with a bunch of Chinese musclemen in the middle of the Tsavo desert. Apart from anything else, he had no beer to offer them.

Fortunately, it did look like Ryan's was closing in faster. But who was that at the wheel? He looked familiar. So did the person leaning forward from the back seat.

Kearney screwed up his eyes and tried to focus.

'Holy SHIT !' he shouted at the lizard, now poised to disappear down its hole and looking back at Kearney over its scaly little shoulder, a satisfied smirk on its face. 'It's that fockin' banker who gave me the bum's rush at that World Bank meeting… and he's got Beatrice fockin' Kinyui with him.

'Oh Jayzus. The bitch has got a gun to Ryan's head.

'Fock.'

OTHER WORKS
by
MARK NEWHAM

COMETH THE YUAN

"Beautifully rendered..." *Guardian*

mark newham

Published in 2014 and set in the not-too-distant future, ***Cometh the Yuan*** is a work of speculative satirical fiction envisaging the not unlikely growing extent of China's influence on the West.

Having already used its economic might to re-colonise most of the developing world, China is now eyeing more challenging targets. Chinese tendrils are already deep into western commerce and industry but that's not enough for China's ambitious leaders. Western political targets are now in China's spotlight and a campaign is launched to infiltrate western seats of power via the services of an unsuspecting multi-billionaire critic of China.

Hong Kong property magnate Harry Wong finds himself hoodwinked into participating in a takeover exercise *par excellence* courtesy of Chinese deceit and Wong's love of cricket. Inculcated into the game at Oxford University, Wong's greatest ambition is to become cricket's new supremo. The man to whom all cricket bows its head. With full Chinese support, Wong's takeover target is none other than Lord's Cricket Ground, the spiritual home of the game. China, it emerges, has confused Lord's with THE Lords – Britain's upper house of parliament.

Can Wong succeed in taking over one of Britain's national treasures? Not if the Marylebone Cricket Club can help it. Almost by accident the bungling historic guardian of Lord's finds itself at the forefront of a battle to combat China's attempt to worm its way into western politics by the back door.

LIMP PIGS

"Unique... Inspiring..." *BBC*

China isn't changing. Well, it is, but not nearly as much as they'd have you believe. And unless real change comes to China soon, a long cold winter of social discontent looms.

Years spent working in the gearbox of China's propaganda machine left Newham unable to conclude otherwise. Attached to two separate Chinese state news agencies between 2003 and 2008, Newham left the country convinced China is politically moribund – as authoritarian, as repressive and as unyielding as it was under Chairman Mao.

Set against China's staggering economic transformation of recent years, Newham says it's this disparity which could ultimately prove China's undoing. The country has become a child with legs growing at unequal rates. Unless something is done soon to address the political/economic inequity, ultimate imbalance is, he believes, inevitable.

Presented in the form of an irreverent memoir-with-attitude of his time working for the Xinhua News Agency and the Beijing Olympics News Service, *Limp Pigs and the Five-Ring Circus* was published in 2011 and ranked **Number One** in Amazon's censorship category for several weeks.

Revised on the inauguration of Xi Jinping as China's president in 2012, *Limp Pigs 2013* is the e-book update of the original.

For sample chapters and availability of both books see:

http://moriartimedia.com/theworks.htm

Lightning Source UK Ltd.
Milton Keynes UK
UKHW01f1600260718
326337UK00001B/49/P

9 780992 662578